A Better Approach *to* PENCIL DRAWING

Frank M. Rines

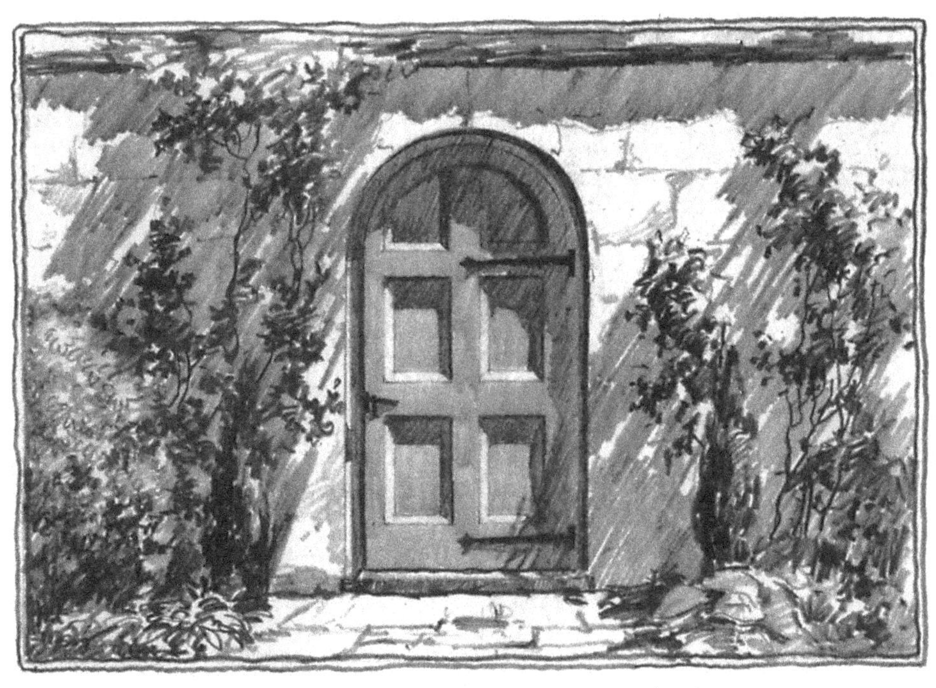

DOVER PUBLICATIONS
Garden City, New York

This Dover edition, first published in 2017, is an unabridged republication, in one volume, of two works originally published by Bridgman Publishers, Inc., Pelham, New York, under the titles *Pencil Drawing* (1940) and *Pencil Sketches* (1935).

Library of Congress Cataloging-in-Publication Data

Names: Rines, Frank M., author illustrator. | Rines, Frank M. Pencil drawing.
 | Rines, Frank M. Pencil sketches.
Title: A better approach to pencil drawing / Frank M. Rines.
Description: Garden City, New York : Dover Publications 2017. | "This
 Dover edition, first published in 2017, is an unabridged republication of
 two works originally published by Bridgman Publishers, Inc., Pelham, New
 York, under the titles Pencil Drawing (1940) and Pencil Sketches (1935).
 The works appear here for the first time as a bound volume."
Identifiers: LCCN 2016052176| ISBN 9780486815916 (paperback) | ISBN 0486815919
Subjects: LCSH: Drawing—Technique. | BISAC: ART / Techniques / Pencil Drawing.
Classification: LCC NC890 .R545 2017 | DDC 741.2/4—dc23 LC record available at
 https://lccn.loc.gov/2016052176

Printed in Canada
81591911   2025
www.doverpublications.com

CONTENTS

PENCIL DRAWING

FOREWORD

By far the most important element of a pencil drawing, and of any drawing or painting in any medium, is a good design or composition. This good composition must be enhanced by accurate drawing. Without these factors no amount of good technique or color will produce a worthwhile picture. When sufficient skill enables the student to combine these essentials and produce an outlined drawing that is interesting in itself, the next step is to develop this outline by adding lights and shadows together with the suggestion of color and texture.

Each medium possesses special characteristics and advantages. Proper handling of the graphite pencils, commonly known as "lead" pencils, produce more varied effects than any of the other black and white media. Some of these effects, together with suggestions on how to obtain them, are presented in the following pages. A serious study of these will, it is hoped, convince even the sceptical, that the possibilities of this medium are almost unlimited. It is, of course, impossible in a book of this size, to approach the subject in any but a more or less "sketchy" manner. In order to get the most satisfactory results, the student should work out for himself as many problems as possible. Conscientious practice cannot be emphasized too strongly.

To produce really good work, the best of materials are an absolute necessity. One of the many advantages of "pencil drawing" is the inexpensiveness of the best materials, and, due to the small amount of equipment, the ease with which it can be taken on either short or prolonged journeys. A list of all the materials needed is herewith presented.

Pencils:—2H, H, F, HB, B, 2B, 3B, 4B. (Any standard make)

Paper:—3 ply *smooth* Strathmore Bristol Board (accept nothing else).

Drawing Board, at least 16 by 20 inches.

Knife or Razor Blade.

Sandpaper Scratcher or Nail File.

1 Kneaded Eraser. 1 Red Eraser.

Plentiful supply of scrap paper (at least 8 x 10 inches).

When working out of doors a strong but light camp stool and a pair of colored glasses are needed—the latter on account of the smooth surface of the paper, which reflects the full glare of the sunlight.

A few thumbtacks and a straight edge (ruler) should be at hand. The Bristol Board comes in sheets 22½ x 28½ inches. If these are cut into fourths a very convenient size is obtained.

LIST of ILLUSTRATIONS and CONTENTS

LIST of ILLUSTRATIONS and CONTENTS

THE OLD SWIMMING HOLE

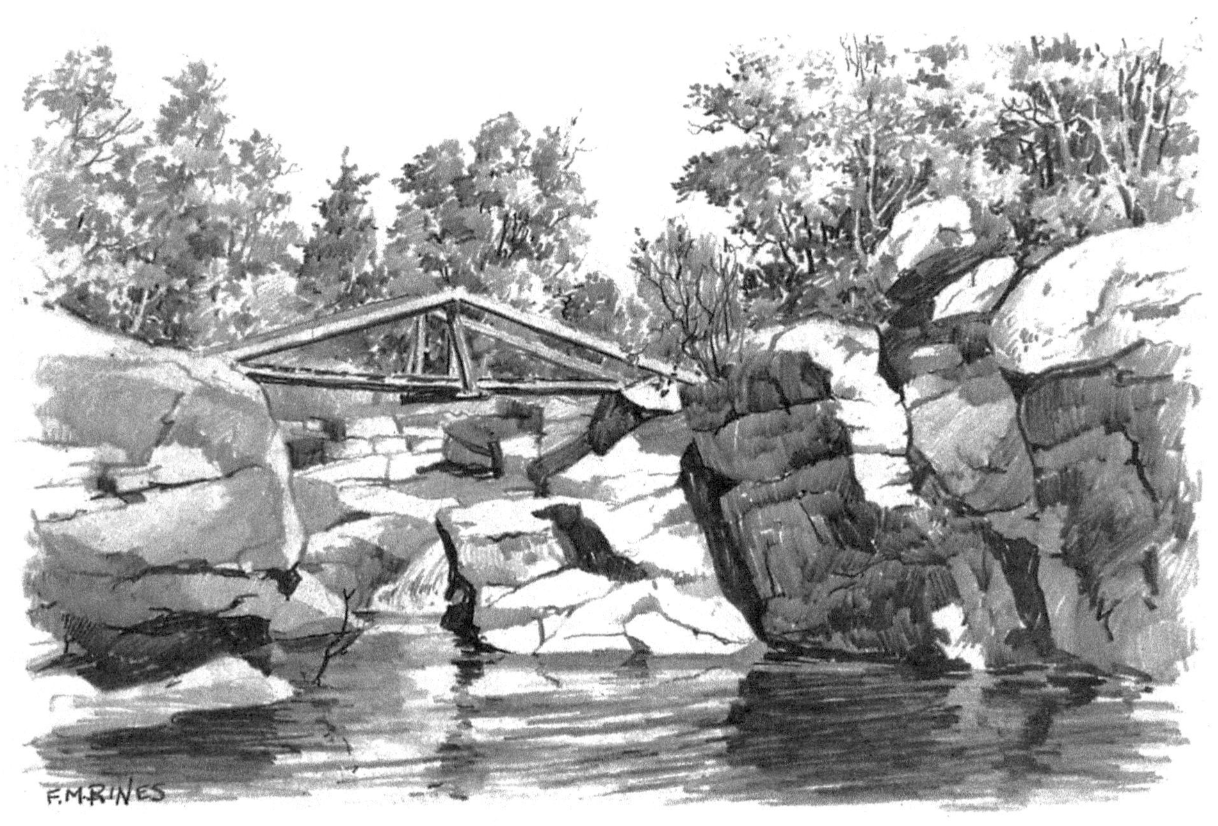

INSTRUCTIONS FOR THE BEGINNER

Sharpen the pencils as shown in the accompanying illustration, except for the one with which the outline is to be made. This latter should have a long, sharp point which can afterwards be worn down like the others. A little experiment- ing will acquaint you with the meaning of the numbers and letters on the different pencils. Always keep an extra sheet of paper under the one upon which you are drawing, in order that the grain of the board will not affect the pencil strokes, which should always be made with a firm, hard pressure (see page thirteen). Use the scrap paper under your hand at all times, both to protect the drawing and to try out the different pencils.

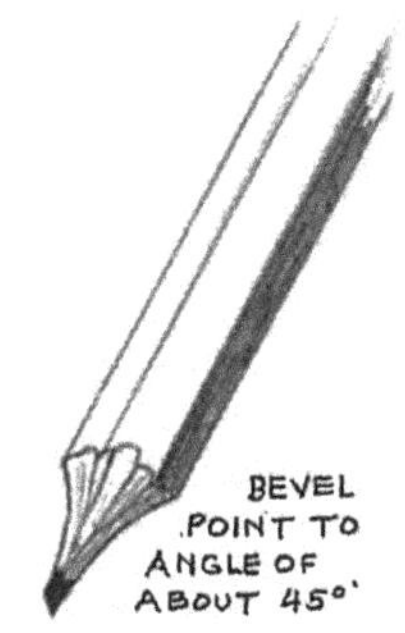

When made on the paper recommended, with the firm pressure described, a pencil drawing does not require any "fixatif" to protect it. A piece of smooth paper (ordinary wrapping paper is ideal) pasted at the top of the drawing, on the back, and folded over the front, will provide ample protection against rubbing, or smudging.

Nothing can take the place of working directly from the actual subject, or "from nature". As this is not always possible, however, drawing from photographs is the next best procedure. Do not attempt to make a literal "copy" of the photograph, but regard it as so much material, from which you will accept and reject, and to which you will add, exactly as you would if working from the same subject in its reality (as explained on page twenty-six). Bear in mind that simplification is the keynote of any successful drawing, whether made from a photograph or out of doors.

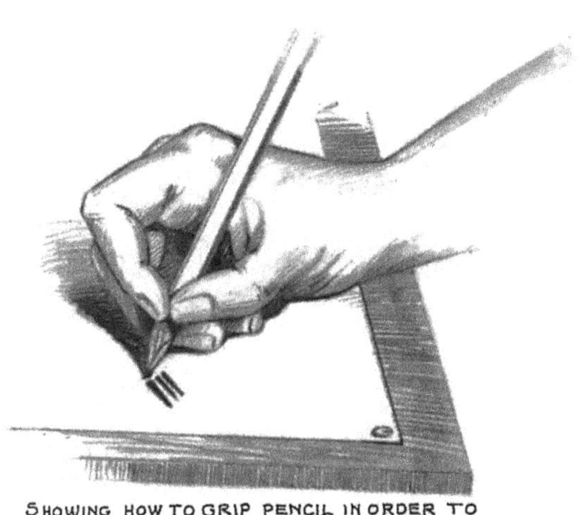
SHOWING HOW TO GRIP PENCIL IN ORDER TO GET FIRM HARD PRESSURE

The tendency of nearly every beginner is to start his composition on too large a scale. Watch out for this, as no drawing will look good if it appears crowded or cramped. The best way is to make, lightly, a border of at least an inch around the sheet before starting to draw, and then try to keep within this space.

It is impossible to do much sketching out of doors, or of landscape subjects, without including trees in the composition. Neglecting to consider them as important as the other elements is a mistake made by many students and professional artists. By far the most satisfactory method is to observe and study trees carefully, until a thorough knowledge of their charac- teristics, anatomy, and individuality is developed.

A faithful performance of this observation will, at the same time, bring about an appreciation and a love for them. Then is the time to commence drawing them; but the study and observation should be continued.

Draw the tree very carefully in outline first. Do not try to draw every branch or clump of foliage exactly as it is, for that would be impossible, but try to design it, at the same time retaining its characteristics. Sometimes these characteristics can be emphasized, but care must be taken not to overdo this (page twenty-one).

After deciding what are the characteristics of the particular tree you are drawing, and after you have very carefully indicated these as much as you can in outline, make the broad strokes of the pencil run in the general direction in which the leaves grow. Curve these strokes, instead of making them straight as you would on a building, and mass them together sometimes, and again allow the individual strokes to be seen.

Since our space is limited, not much can be said about trees here. However, in my book "Design and Construction in Tree Drawing" (Bridgman) the subject is more fully treated.

CENTER OR FOCAL POINT

ALWAYS avoid having any dominant lines or edges come in the exact horizontal or vertical center. In A the farther corner of the building and the horizon line do this. Observe, in B, how the position of the building and the horizon line have been shifted.

Never have any object which is capable of movement (such as boats, figures, animals, etc.) facing directly out of, or away from the center of interest. If this is done, the eyes are pulled away from this center or focal point.

Note how the boats, which in A both point outward, have been rearranged in B so that they direct the attention toward the center.

Also avoid crowding too much interest into the corners where it will be entirely disconnected from the rest of the composition. The small boat which in A seems to be an afterthought and pulls the gaze away from the building, the subject of the picture, is placed in B so that it not only points inward, but becomes part of a unified composition by means of the reflection tones.

In C, besides further illustrating the importance of avoiding the center, the roadway starts in one corner of the picture, drawing the attention toward the right and out of the composition without focusing the attention at all on the trees which are the subject. In D the eyes follow the roadway and are led right up to the trees. Also, the very uninteresting triangle, in the lower right corner of C, becomes in D, a more pleasing shape.

In E, the two tree trunks have been placed so that they hide dominant lines of the houses. Such placement causes the composition to appear too formal and obvious. Note how much more informal F becomes because these trunks have been drawn in slightly different positions. Such placing is equally important when drawing masts of boats and when adding accessories such as figures, etc.

As a similar example, notice the tip of the mast and its relation to the ridgepole in A. Now observe the change made in B by simply extending the tip a trifle.

It is well to bear in mind that, as a rule, uneven numbers—one, three, five, etc.— make for better composition than even numbers. Hence, three boats in B instead of the two in A, the three trees in F in place of the two in E, and the one large tree in C and D. While not a hard and fast rule like most of the others spoken of here, compositions generally are improved when this proportion is followed.

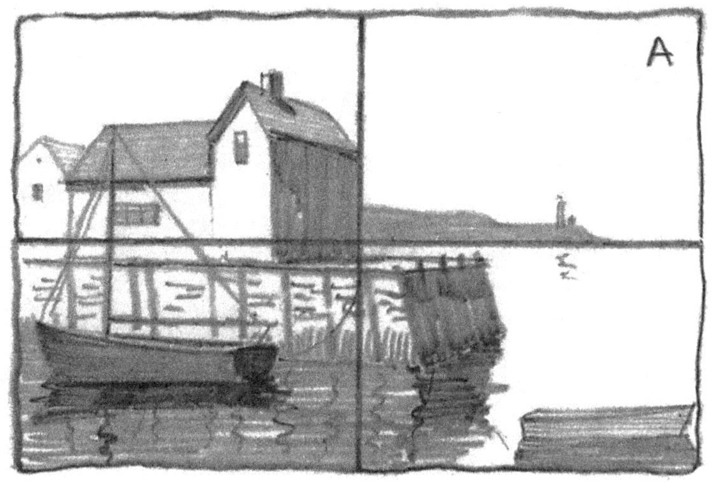 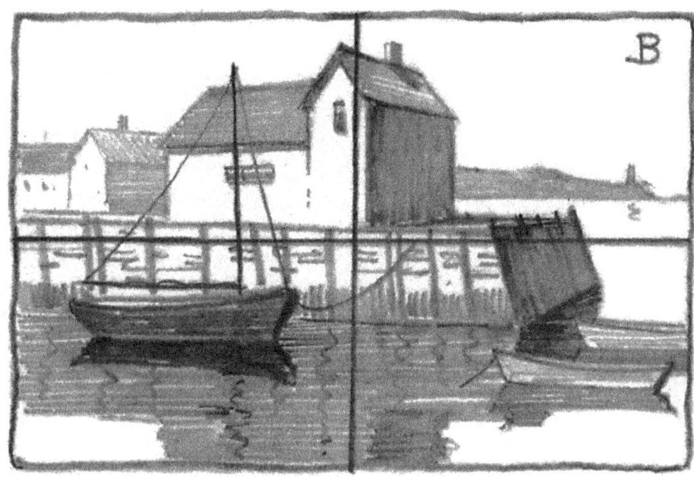

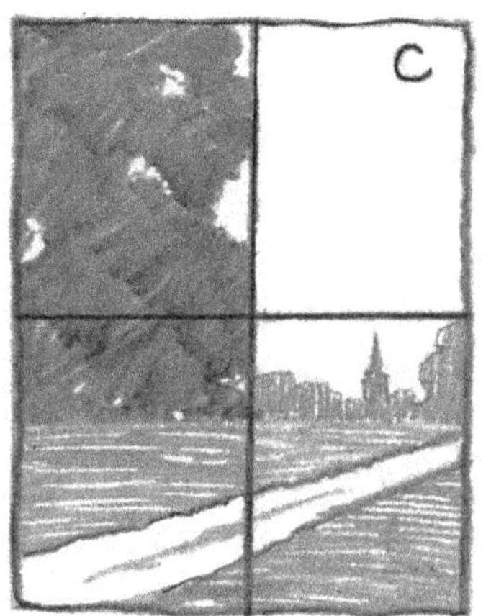 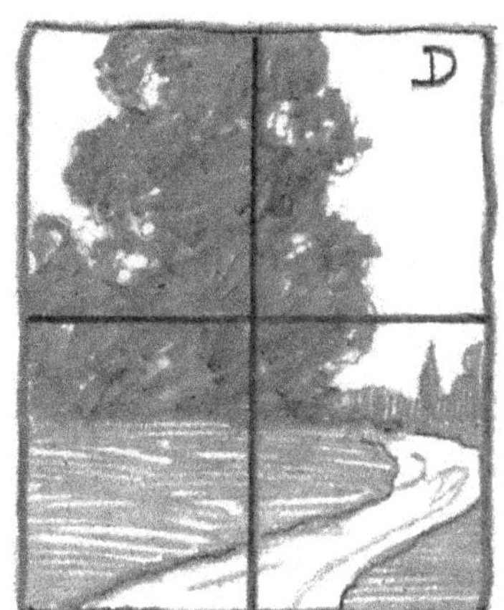 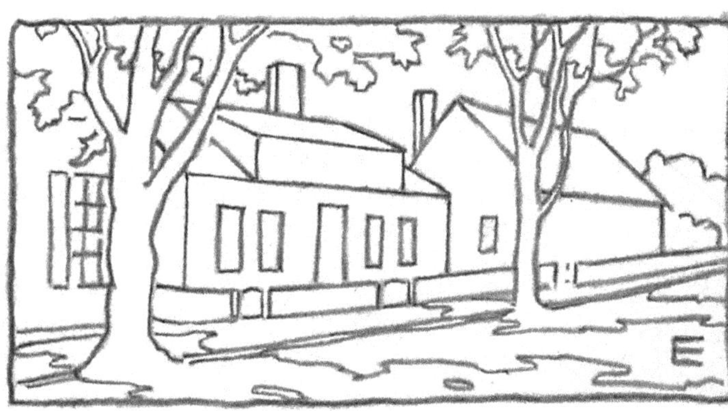

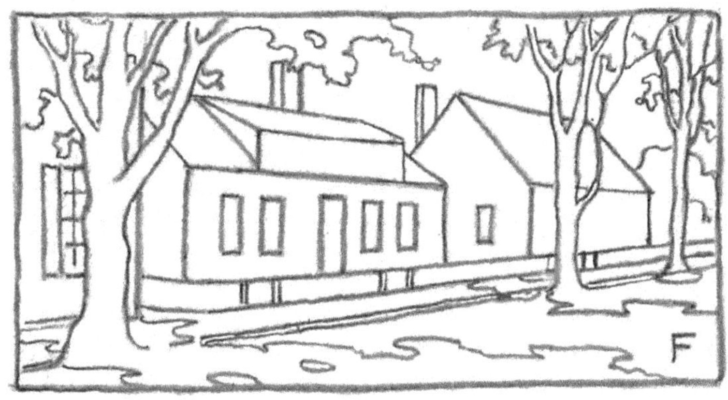

In E and F the street, running diagonally across the picture, might seem to violate the principle of C and D. The fact that it is so broken up with shadows, however, offsets any such effect as occurs in C.

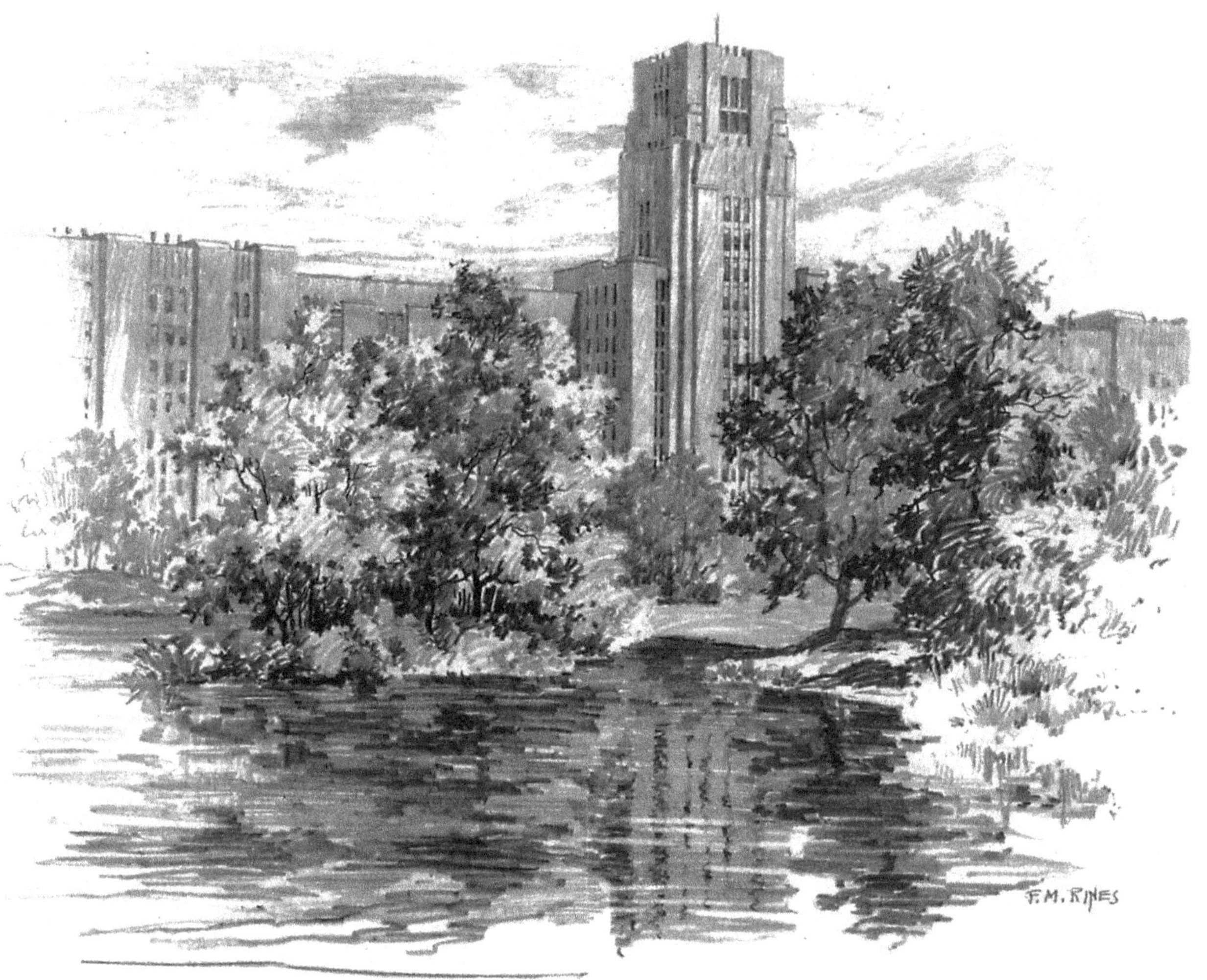

PERSPECTIVE

WHEN complete books have been written about perspective, it can be readily understood that the subject can only be broached here. These few examples will, however, give an idea of some of the governing principles. Nearly everyone realizes that the farther away an object is, the smaller it appears. Observation helps the artist to determine the angle of vanishing lines and the proportionate size of diminishing objects, but a working knowledge of the theories of perspective forms a valuable aid to such observation.

In many magazines and newspapers innumerable photographs of houses, street scenes, and buildings may be found. If you will, with a straight edge and a soft pencil, follow to their conclusion the various lines and edges in these pictures, your understanding of these principles will be greatly increased.

The horizon, or eye level, is exactly what the name implies—i.e.—the level of the eye when viewing the object. This eye level, therefore, will be raised or lowered as one's position becomes higher or lower. Every horizontal line, if projected far enough, will eventually cross this eye level line. Every horizontal line, IN THE SAME PLANE, or THE SAME SURFACE, will, when projected, meet this eye level line at the SAME POINT, called the VANISHING POINT.

Obviously, then, when the eye level line is somewhere between the upper and lower edges of a plane or surface, some of these lines will have to slope upward and some downward. Reference to the accompanying diagrams will make this clearer. Not only will all the lines in this plane vanish to this one point, but all the lines in every PARALLEL plane will vanish to this SAME POINT.

In the case of almost every building or similar object, the two sides or surfaces that we see from any one station point are at right angles to each other.

Therefore, whatever is true of all the horizontal lines of one plane is true, in the reverse, of all the similar lines in the plane which is at right angles to it. This means that the lines in this second plane will vanish to a point at the OPPOSITE end of the eye level line. The rapidity, or acuteness of the angle at which they vanish is determined by the angle at which this plane is with the station point of the observer.

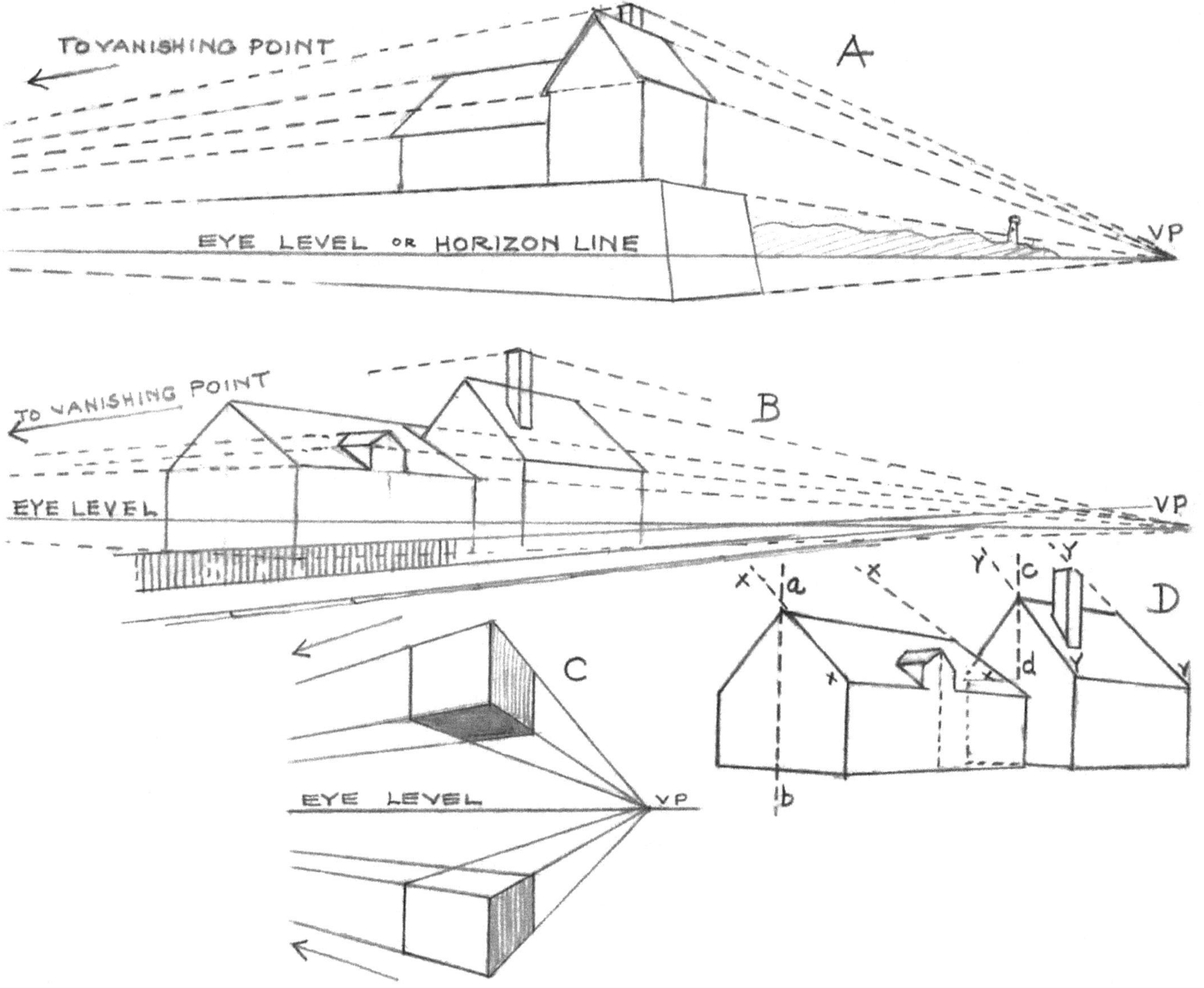

There can be but ONE EYE LEVEL LINE in any picture, and only ONE VANISHING POINT for all PARALLEL PLANES. There will be, however, as many vanishing points, all on the same eye level line, as there are planes at different angles to one another.

While only one of the vanishing points is shown in these diagrams, the approximate locations of the other vanishing points are indicated.

There is one exception to the above statements. If the observer is stationed exactly in front of an object, so that only one of its four vertical planes can be seen, the perspective then becomes so subtle that it can be ignored. Such views are used a great deal in architectural renderings, and are known as "elevation views". As they are not, as a rule, "artistic," and therefore not a wise selection for a freehand treatment, further reference to them can be dismissed here.

With the foregoing statements in mind, diagram A should be obvious. B is an illustration of the problem encountered in A, complicated by the addition of a fence and sidewalk. Since this building is situated on sloping ground, that is, since the ground is *not horizontal*, and the fence is built in relation to the land rather than to the building, the rule for vanishing horizontal lines can not be applied to it. The width of these will, of course, diminish as they recede, but not in accordance with the eye level line.

Diagram C should need no further explanation.

Diagram D illustrates two new principles. They still relate to the fact that everything appears to diminish as it recedes. The lines a b and c d divide the gable ends into two parts, the width of the nearer parts being greater, BECAUSE THEY ARE NEARER TO THE EYE. For the same reason the dormer window is slightly more distant from the nearer corner of the building than from the farther corner.

We know, of course, that in reality the eaves and ridgepole are the same length. Yet the ridgepole is more distant than the eave. Therefore, the lines x must eventually converge, as must the two lines y, in order to make the ridgepole lengths slightly shorter than the eaves. These two principles are more often neglected than any of the other principles of perspective.

PENCIL TECHNIQUE

THE examples shown here are only a few of an infinite number of strokes and combinations of strokes that can be obtained by a skillful manipulation of the range of pencils given under the list of materials.

Constant practice makes perfect, in pencil drawing as in every other worth while accomplishment. Experiment—try out for yourself as many strokes and variations of strokes as possible, and practice these as frequently as you can.

By doing this, you will gradually become less and less conscious of your pencil as a tool, leaving your thoughts more free to concentrate on the other elements of the picture.

Remember to keep the leads well flattened by use of the scratcher or nail file and to always bear down as firmly as possible. Even then the pressure will vary somewhat, but this slight inequality of tone will not, as a rule, be objectionable.

Make every stroke *directly* — never "scumble", or *go back over a stroke the second time.* To get the "wash" effects, or flat tones, apply the strokes closely together. In this way, the individual strokes are more or less lost. When the desired result is detail, simply keep the strokes more separated. Only by strict observance of this rule will the work appear crisp and sparkling.

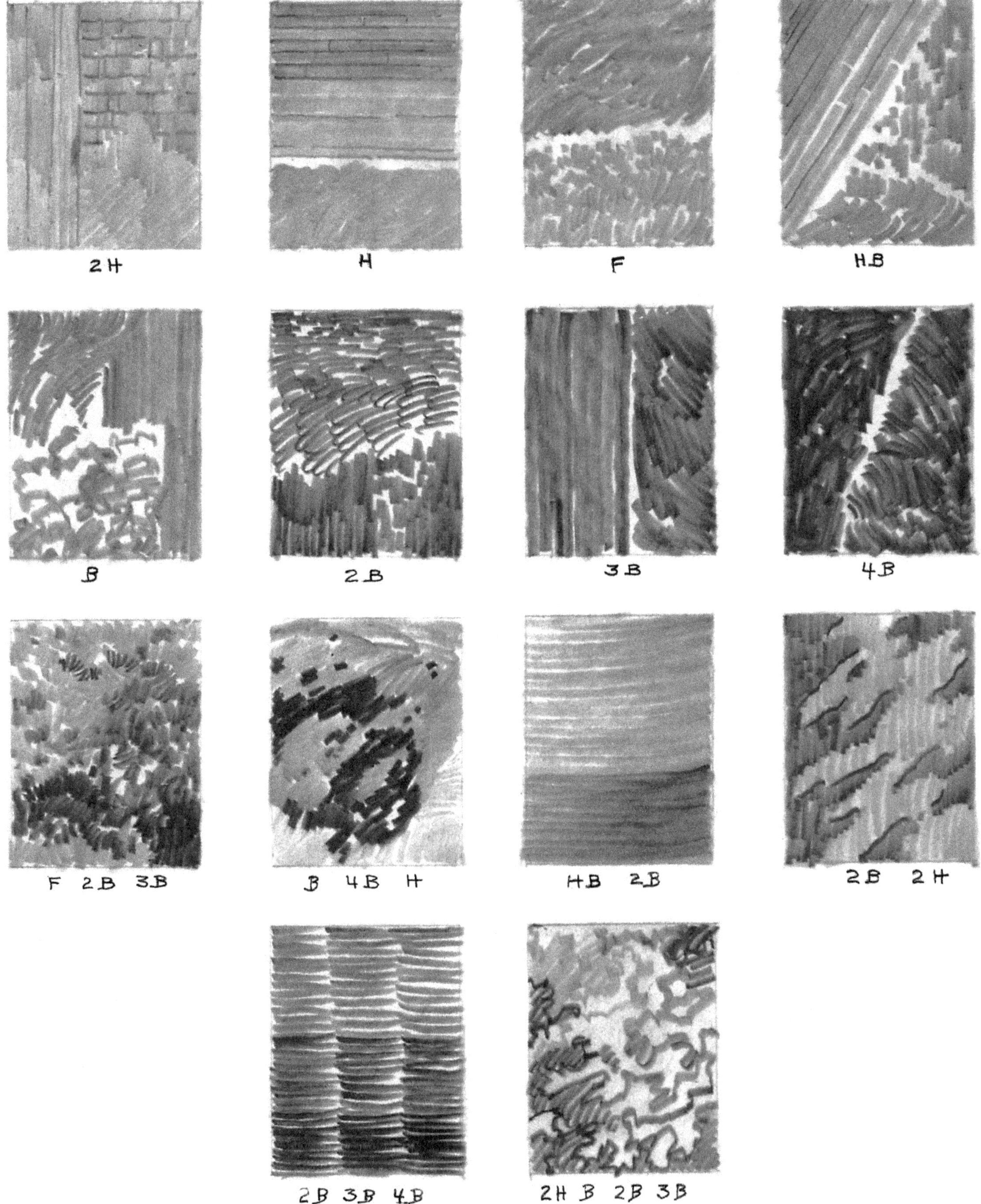

2 H
H
F
H.B
B
2 B
3 B
4 B
F 2 B 3 B
B 4 B H
H.B 2 B
2 B 2 H
2 B 3 B 4 B
2 H B 2 B 3 B

THE COUNTRY LANE

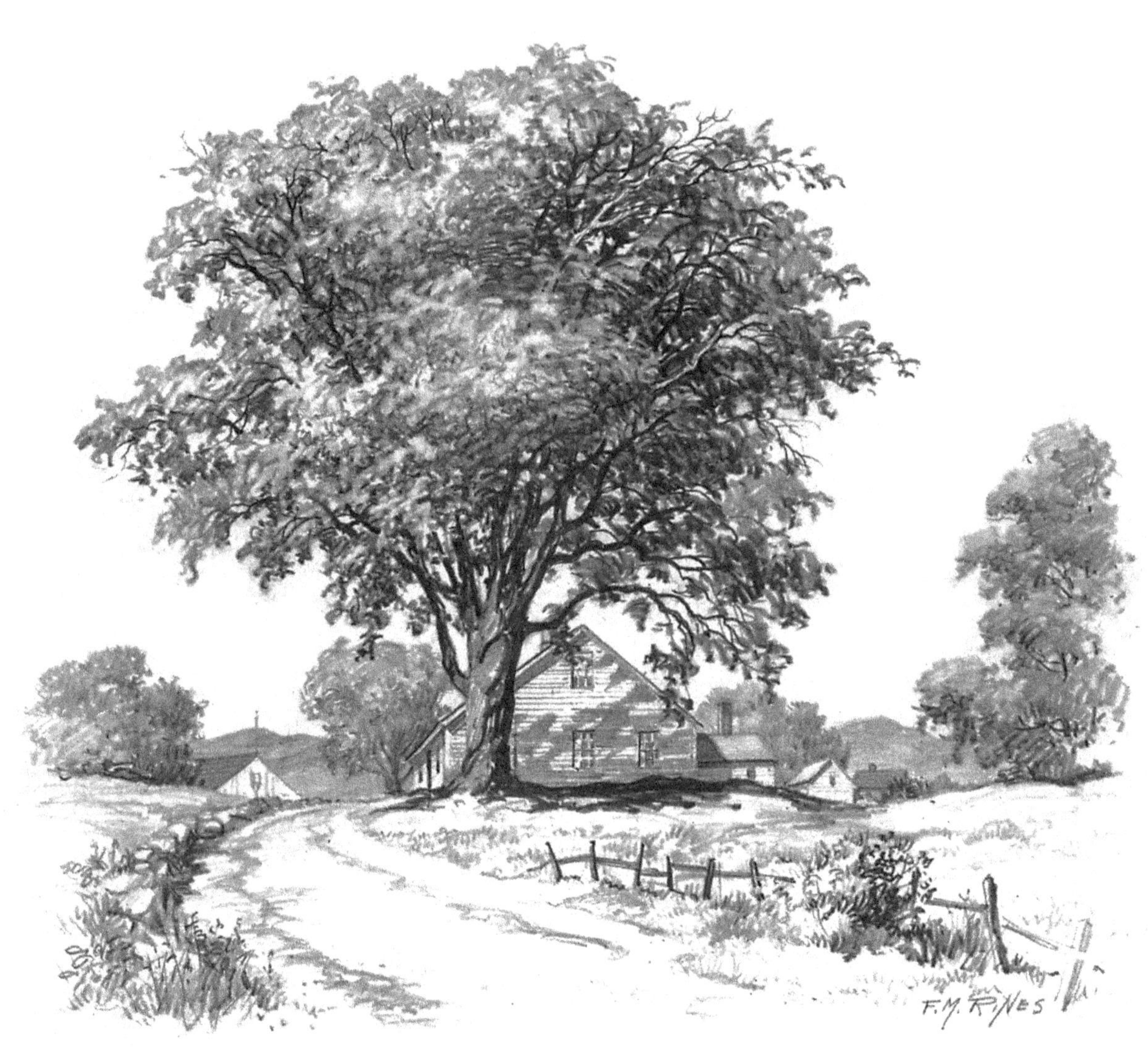

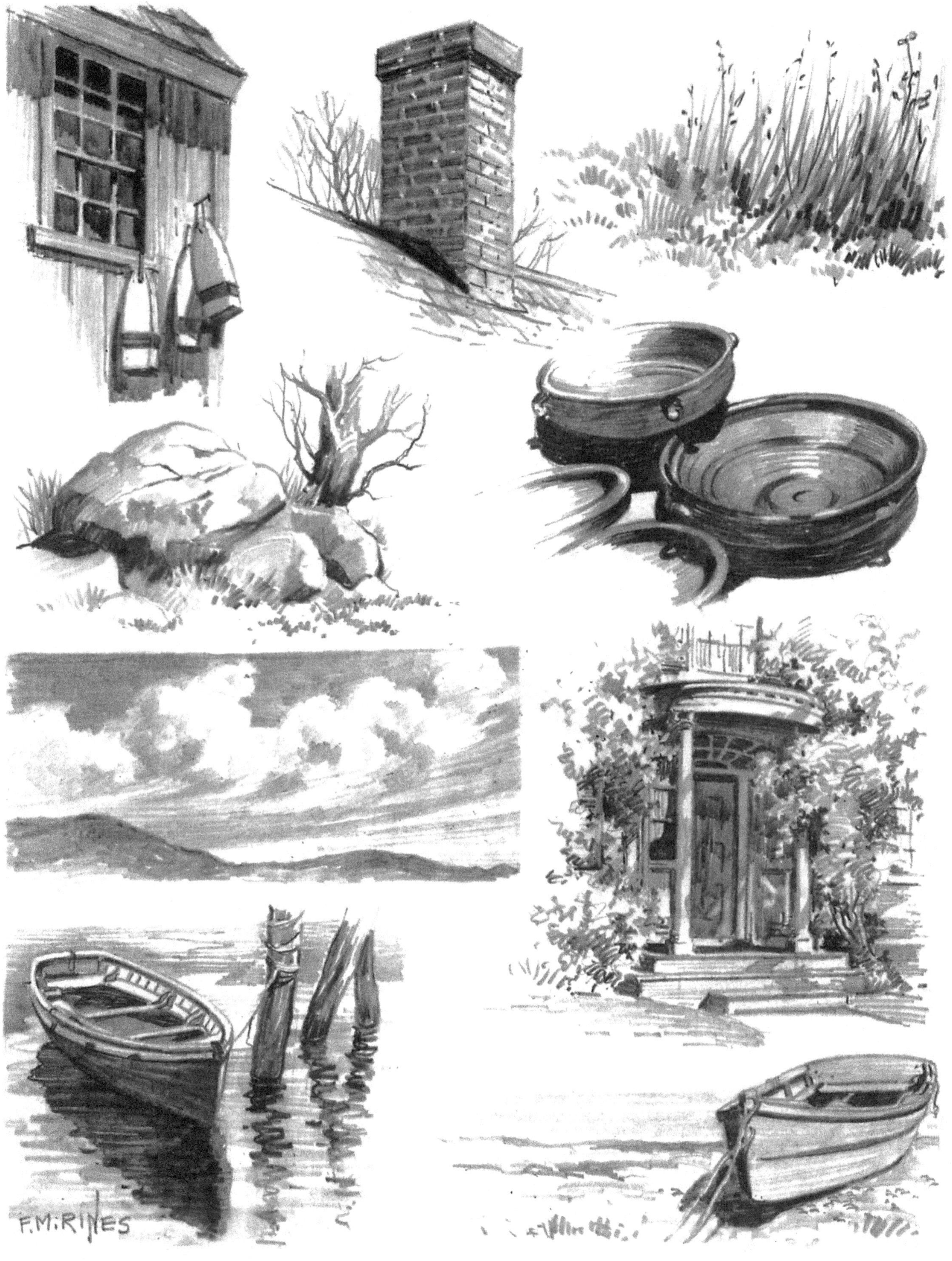

F.M.RINES

PENCIL TEXTURE

THIS outline, like the other outline drawings in this book, had to be made heavier in order to reproduce. The point to be emphasized is the importance of having every-thing carefully planned before any rendering is done.

Cover up the boat with your finger and note how the composition loses much of its interest. Try to visualize it placed somewhere to the left of the center line, and notice how heavy the composition would then appear on that side.

The change of texture on the shadow side of the building helps to break up what would otherwise be a monotonous expanse.

Naturally, in the process of rendering, a few variations from the original outline are introduced in order to enhance the effect, e.g., the few bare twigs in the bush in front of the building, a few suggestions of grass, etc.

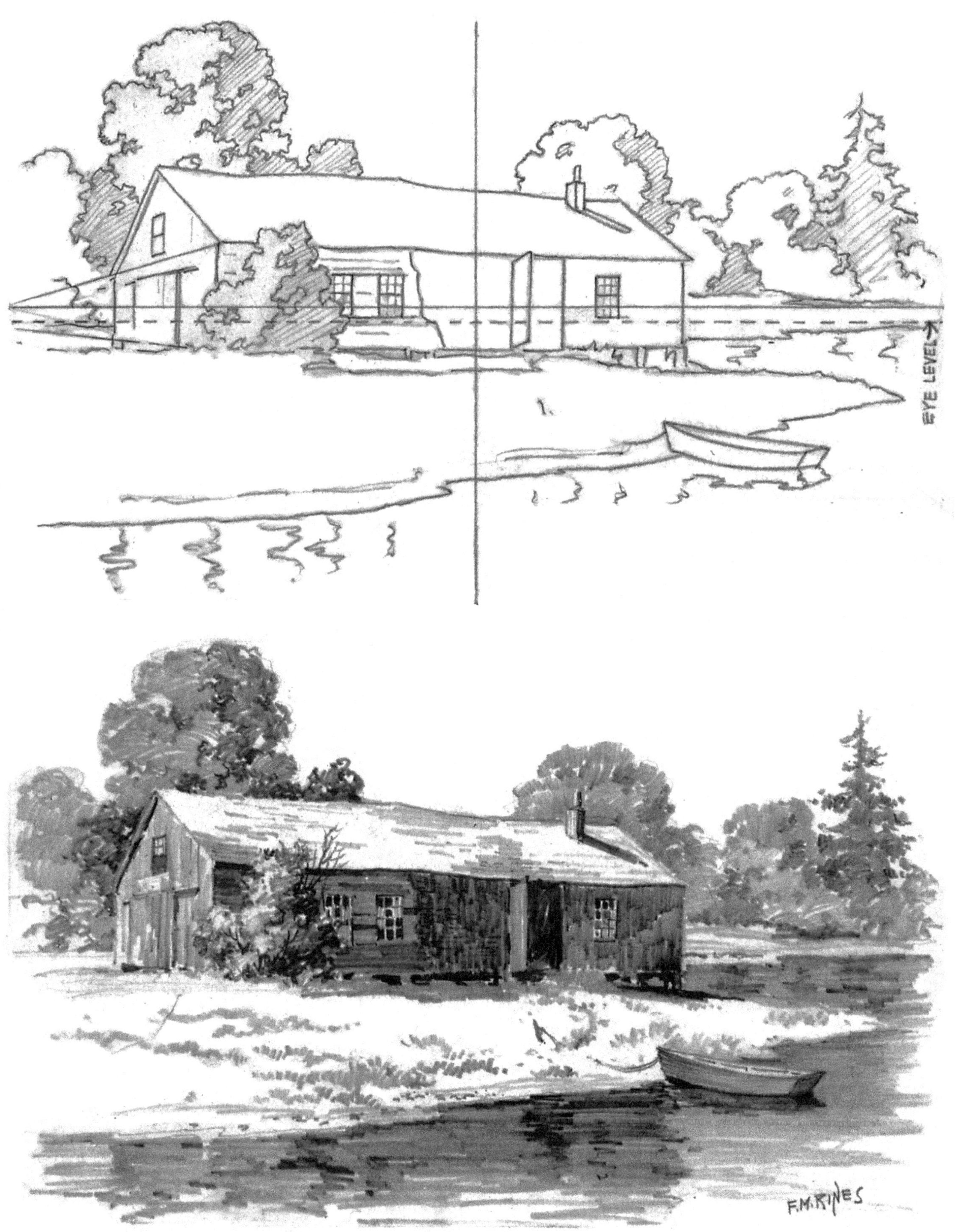

EYE LEVEL
F.M.RINES

STEPS IN PENCIL RENDERING

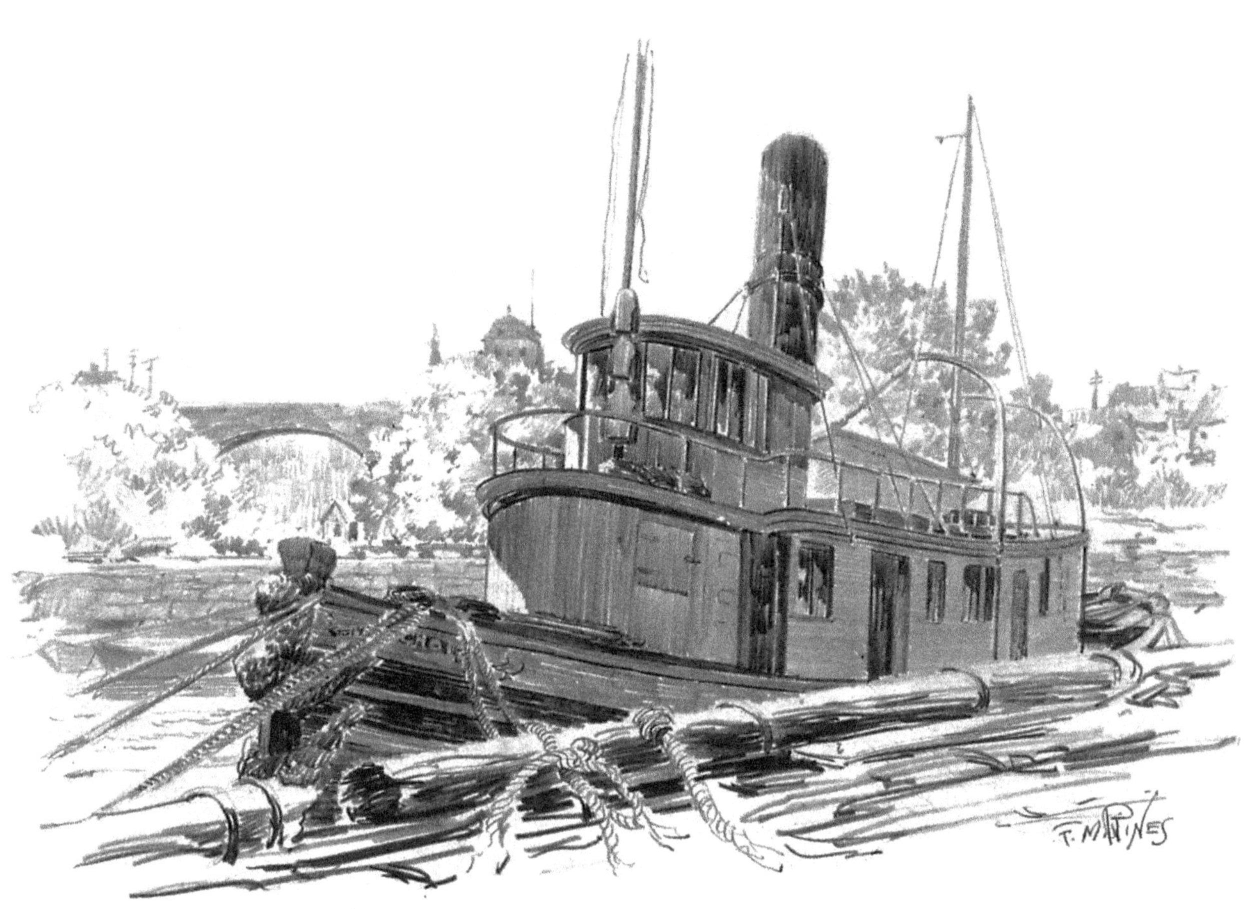

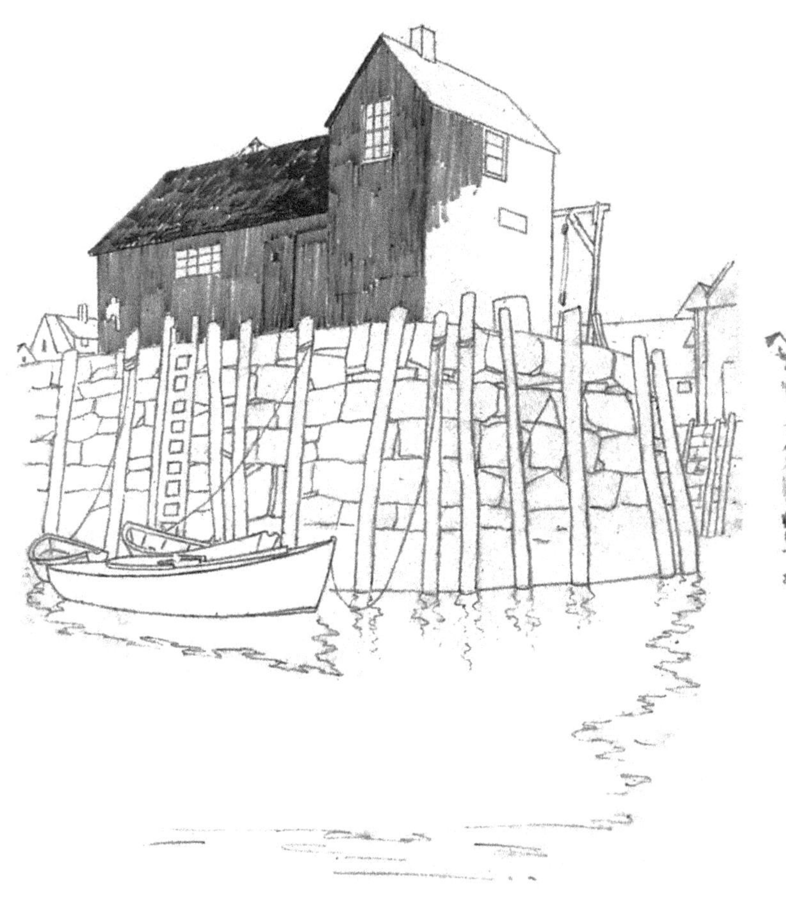

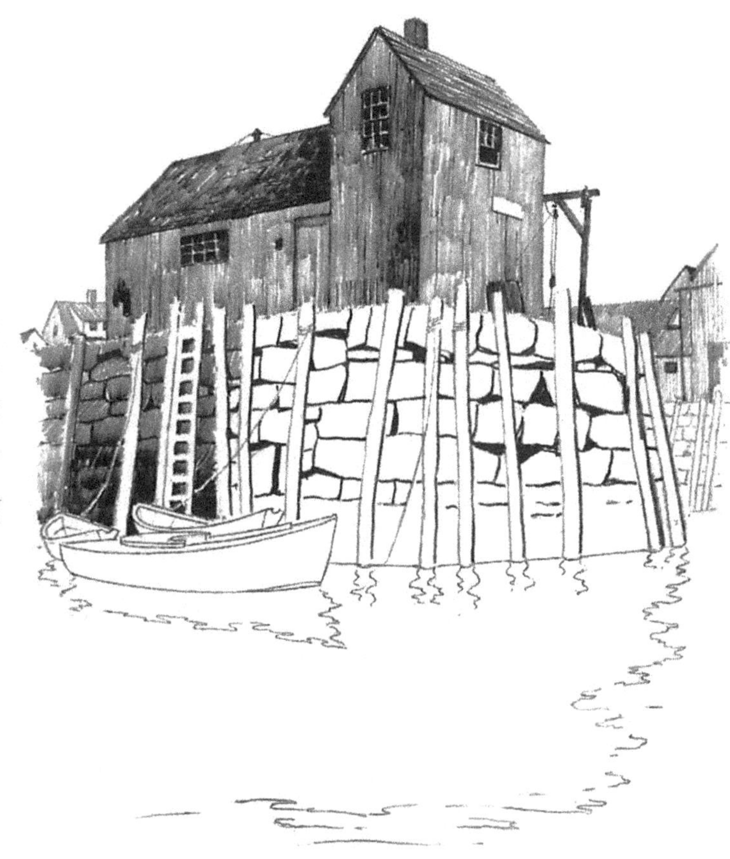

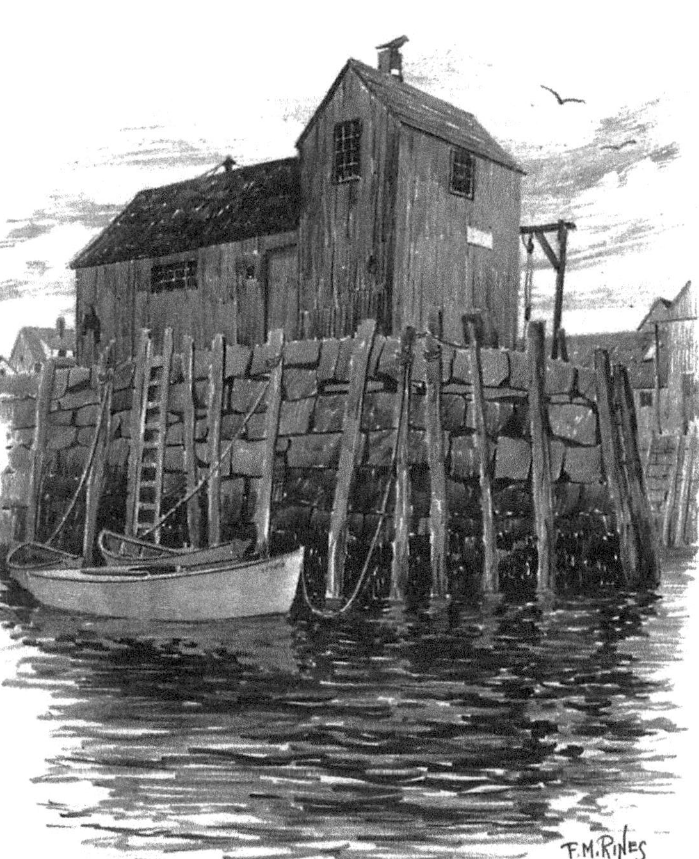

THESE incomplete drawings serve as an illustration of the progressive steps in producing the finished drawing opposite.

After making the careful outline, render the vertical walls of the building with an HB for the side and an F for the front. Make the dark roof next, using a 2B and then the lighter roof with an F, turned slightly edgewise, to make a more lined effect. Then add the accents of the boards and shingles with the sharp edge of the HB, and then the windows, etc., with the 2B. Use an H pencil for the buildings in the background.

Outline heavily with a 2B or 3B (according to the amount of pressure) the shapes of the stones and fill in solidly the crevices between the stones. Next tone the stones with the HB for the light values and a 3B or 4B for the seaweed at the waterline, leaving the piles until the stonework is done. Then tone the piles.

Render the water next, with a B and a 3 or 4B, using a very free stroke.

Leave the boats until the water is finished. Notice that while the individual strokes in the water are not mechanically straight, the general effect is horizontal.

On the boats, let the strokes follow the contour of the boards.

The clouds and seagulls are added last of all.

This drawing is an example of one of the few compositions that are effective in pencil on a cloudy day. The bulky silhouette against the sky takes the place, in a measure, of the contrast of light and shade in the other drawings in this book.

TREE CONSTRUCTION

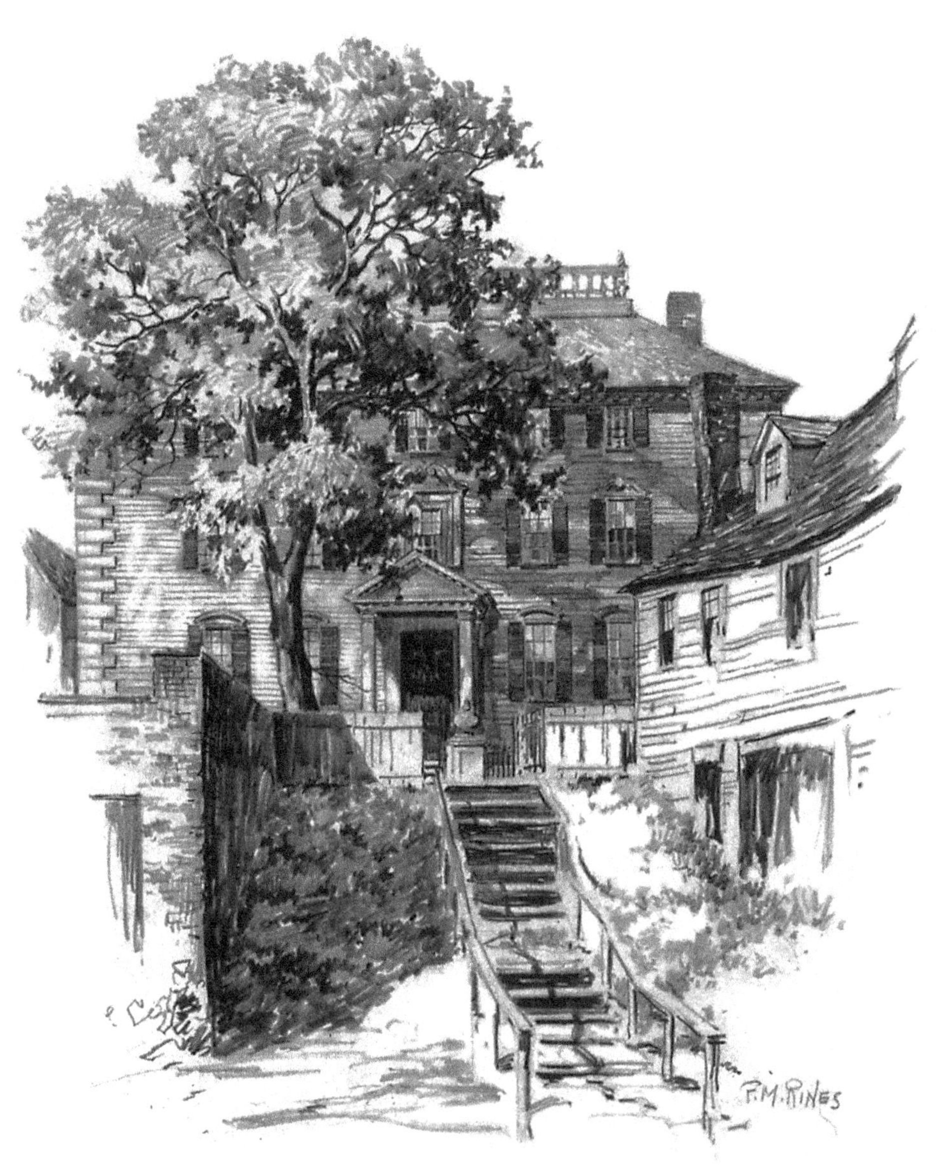

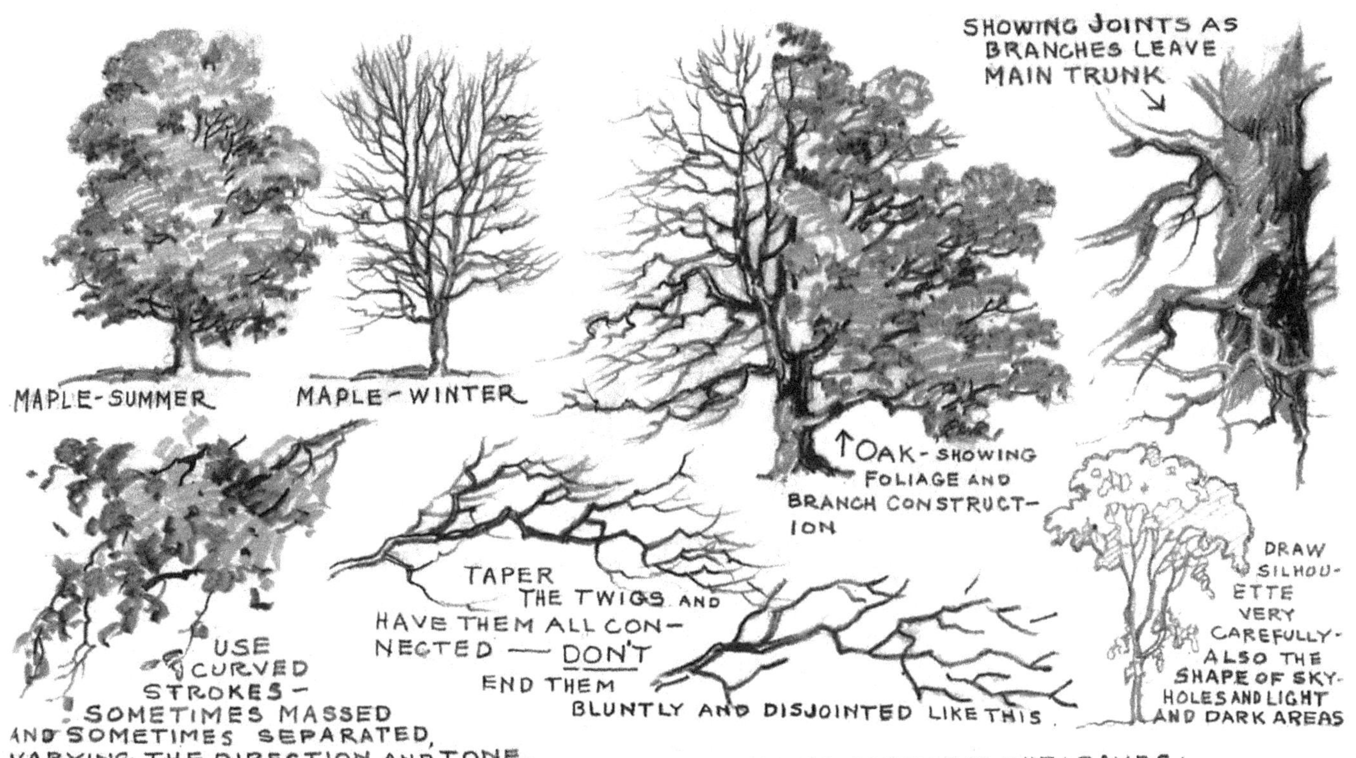

SHOWING JOINTS AS BRANCHES LEAVE MAIN TRUNK
MAPLE-SUMMER
MAPLE-WINTER
OAK-SHOWING FOLIAGE AND BRANCH CONSTRUCTION
USE CURVED STROKES - SOMETIMES MASSED AND SOMETIMES SEPARATED, VARYING THE DIRECTION AND TONE.
TAPER THE TWIGS AND HAVE THEM ALL CONNECTED - DON'T END THEM BLUNTLY AND DISJOINTED LIKE THIS
DRAW SILHOUETTE VERY CAREFULLY - ALSO THE SHAPE OF SKY-HOLES AND LIGHT AND DARK AREAS
DRAW FOLIAGE FIRST - BRANCHES LAST - MAKING THEM SUPPORT THE LEAVES.

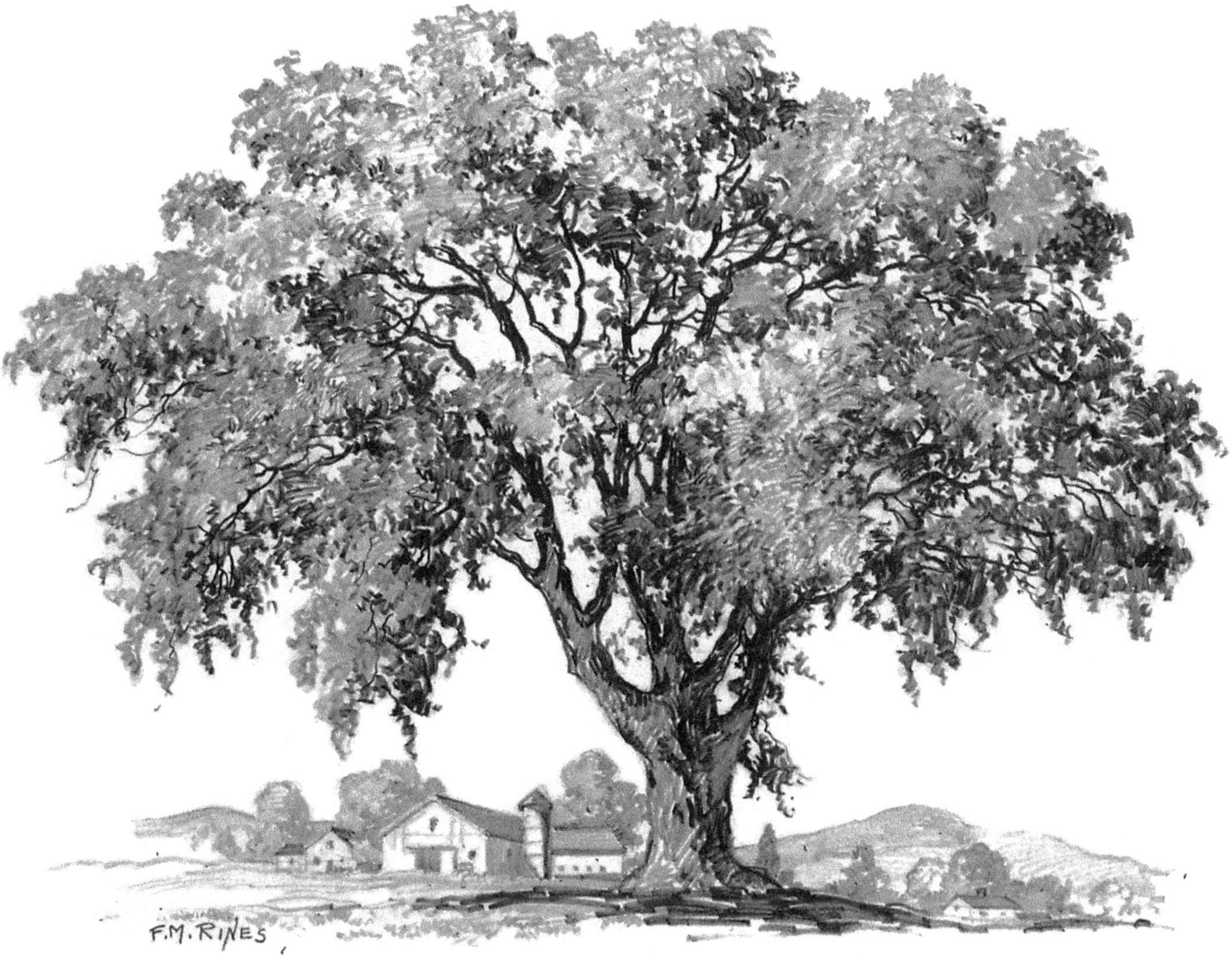

F.M. RINES

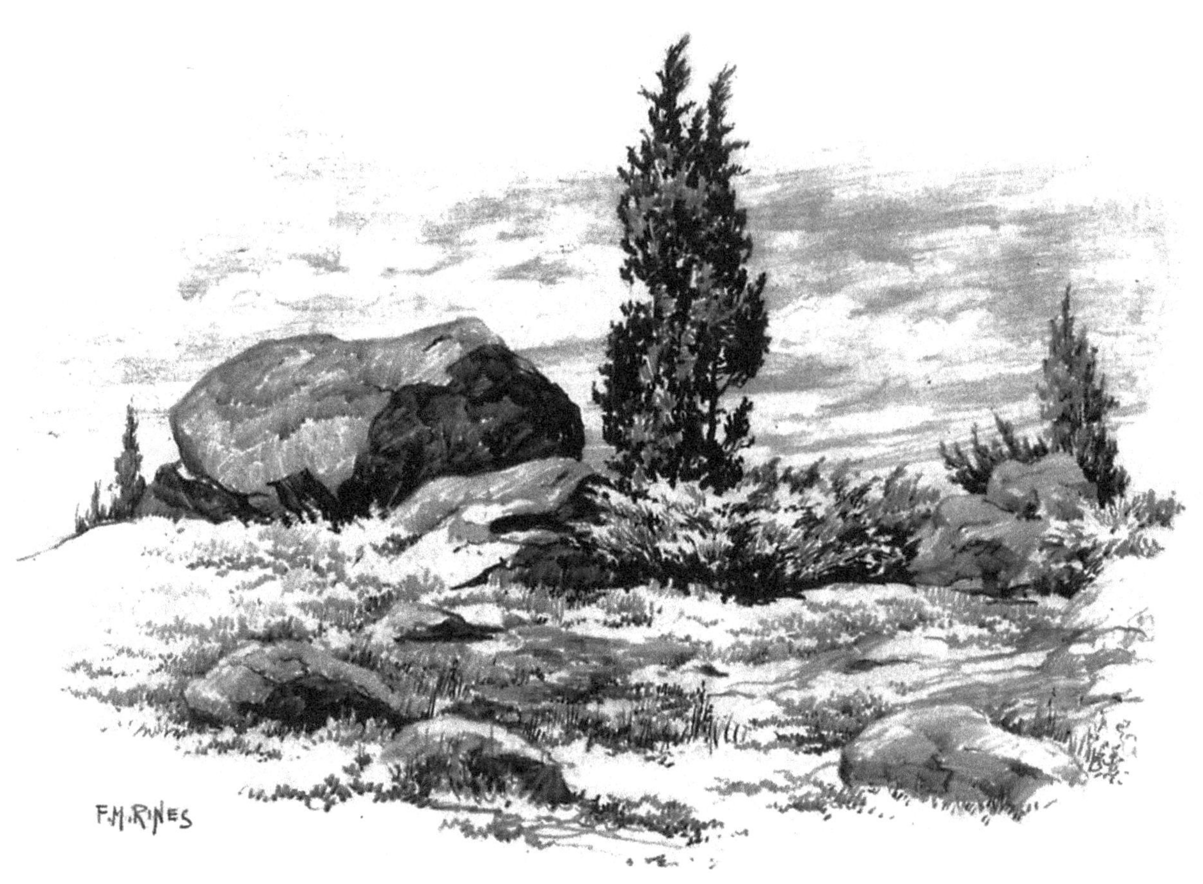

^{F.M.RINES}

COMPLETING THE SKETCH

This illustrates how, after the subject has been carefully drawn in outline, as shown on page seventeen, the entire background of the clapboards on the shadow end of the building is worked around the silhouette of the shrubbery. The softening touches are then added to the shrubbery, as in the completed drawing below. In this manner you can decide just how much or how little modeling the foliage requires.

The upper part of the gable end in shadow has been left unfinished in order to illustrate the guide lines which indicate the perspective or direction of the clapboard strokes.

This upper sketch is reproduced the actual size of the original drawing.

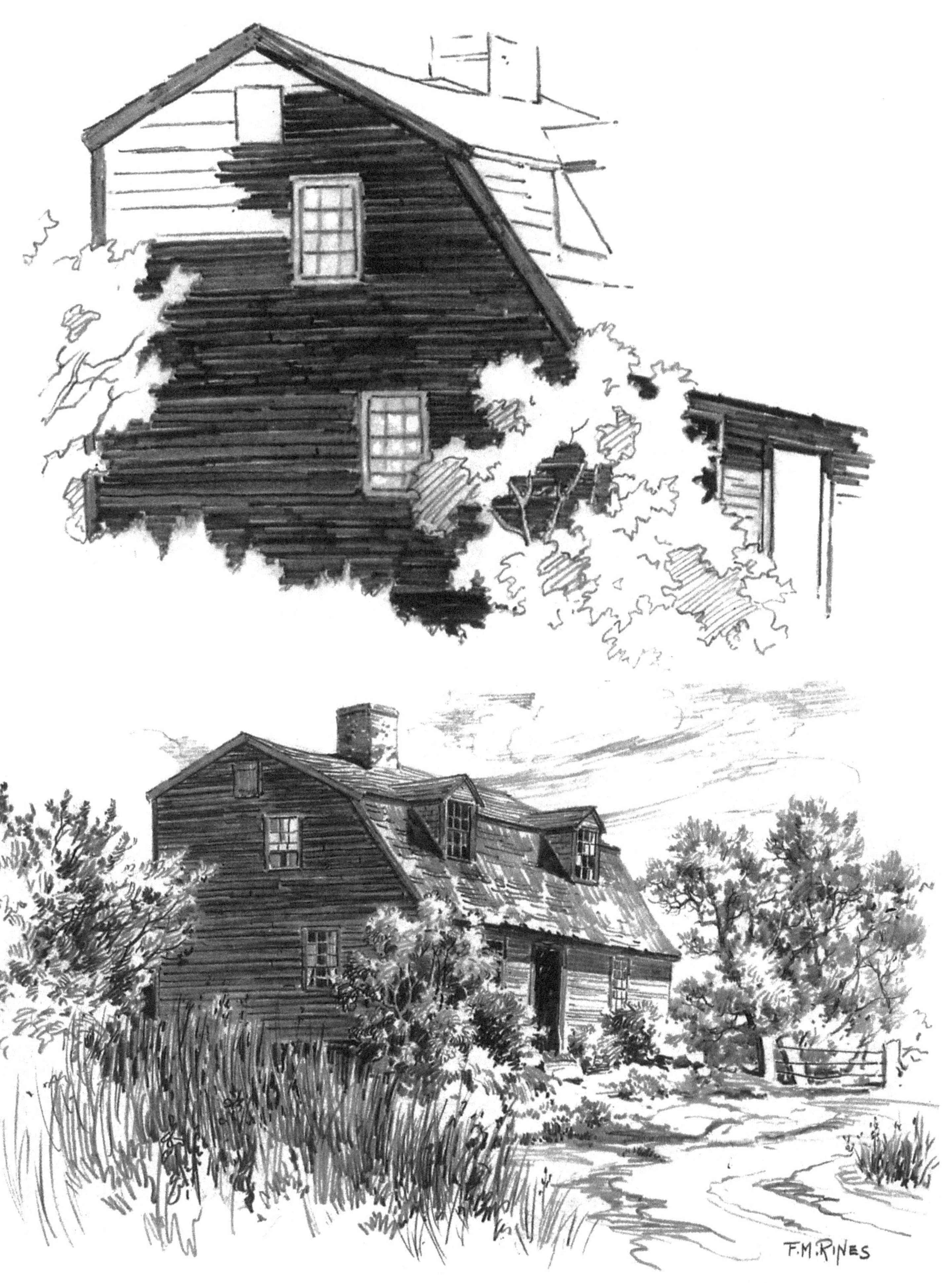

F.M.RINES

THE COVERED BRIDGE

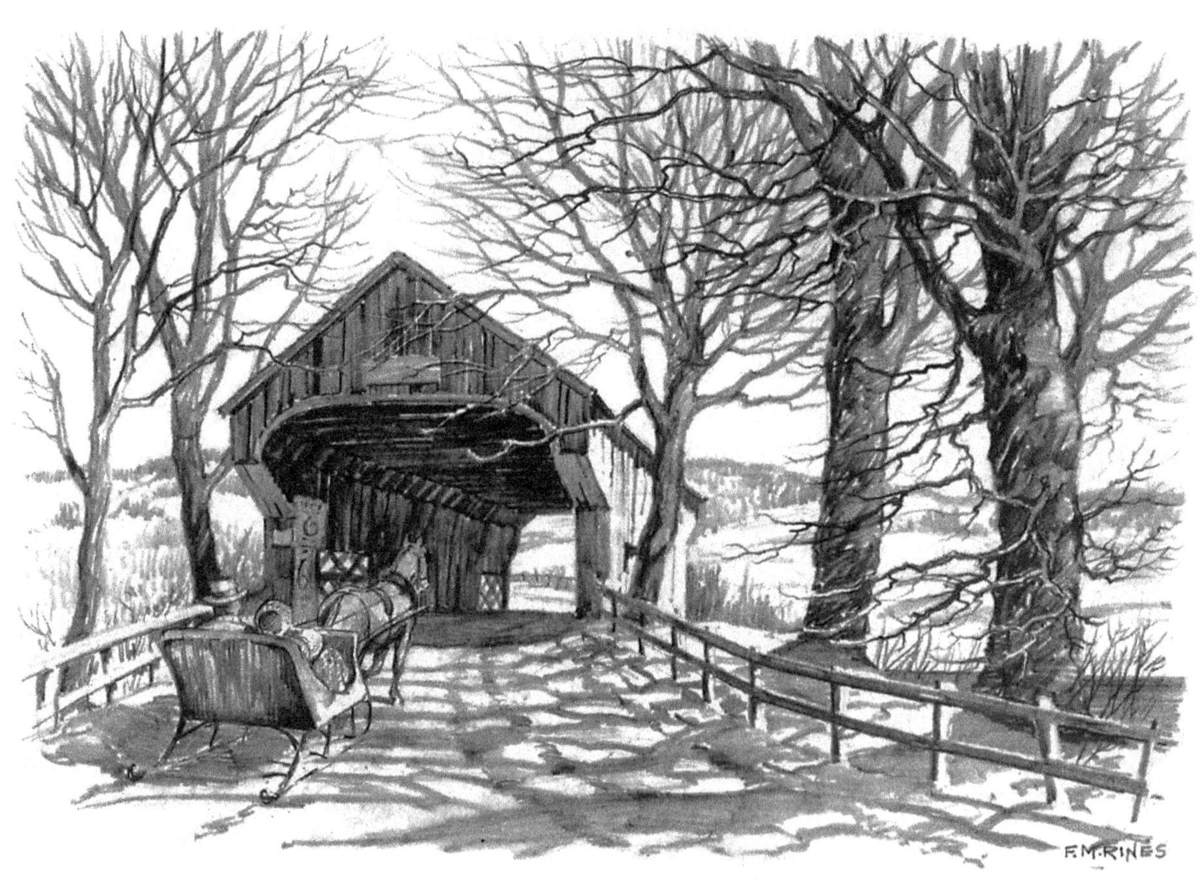

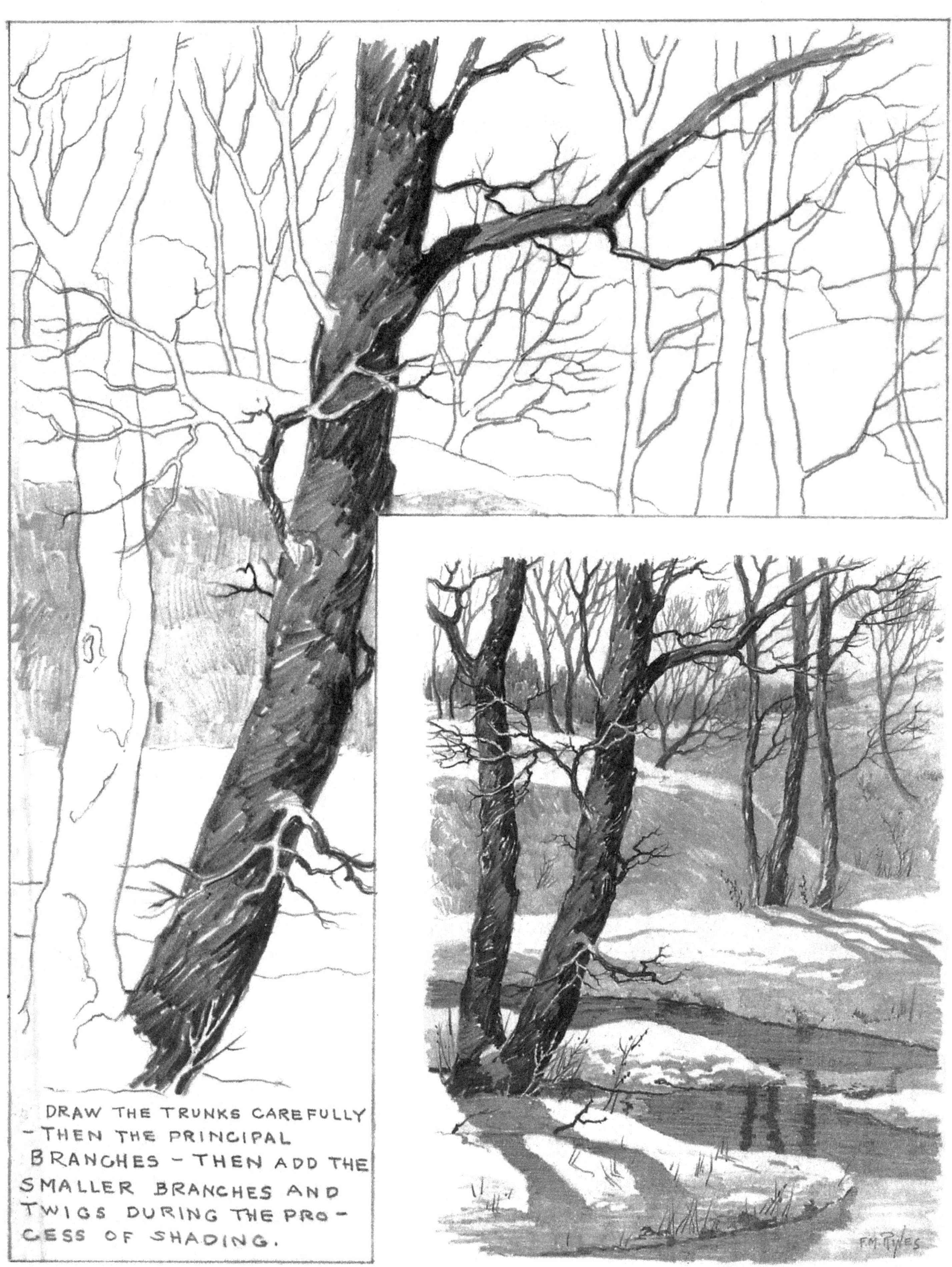
DRAW THE TRUNKS CAREFULLY
- THEN THE PRINCIPAL
BRANCHES - THEN ADD THE
SMALLER BRANCHES AND
TWIGS DURING THE PRO-
CESS OF SHADING.
F.M. Rines

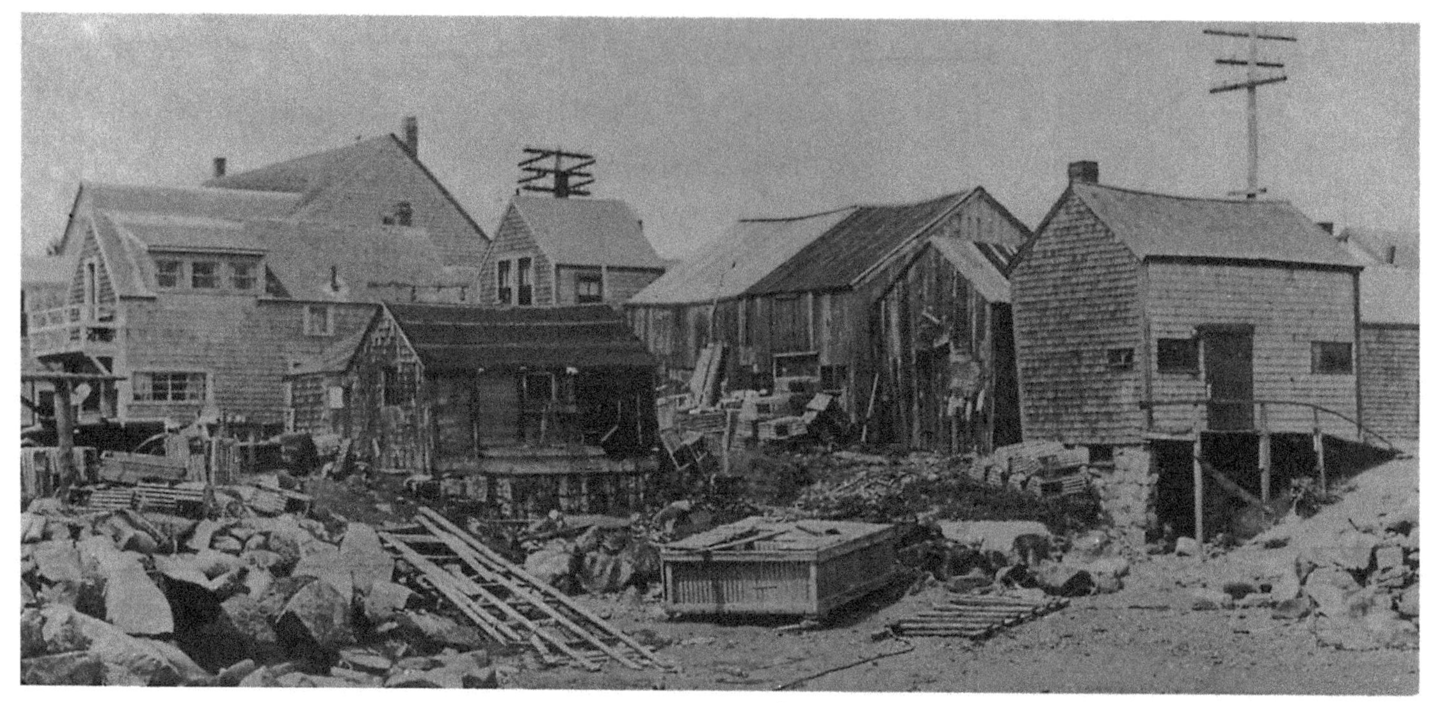

SKETCHING

This photograph was taken in order to show the conglomeration of material that often exists when we are looking for sketchable subjects. The drawing shows one of several compositions that can be made from such material. It emphasizes the point that an artist "copies" from his subject only what he desires, eliminating and transposing the rest, and introducing other objects as he feels the need for them.

The shack with the tarred paper roof has been moved toward the right, eliminating some of the expanse of the building with the long, broken roof line. This building has been drawn, as it is in the photograph, slightly out of perspective. In reality the building is tilted because the sills have partially rotted away. This effect has been retained in the drawing in order to make the shack look old and weatherbeaten.

This scene was purposely taken with almost no sunlight and shadow effects. In the drawing the lighting has been changed, thereby obtaining a much more interesting result. The introduction of the steps, lobster traps, etc., supply notes of secondary interest, which the photograph lacks.

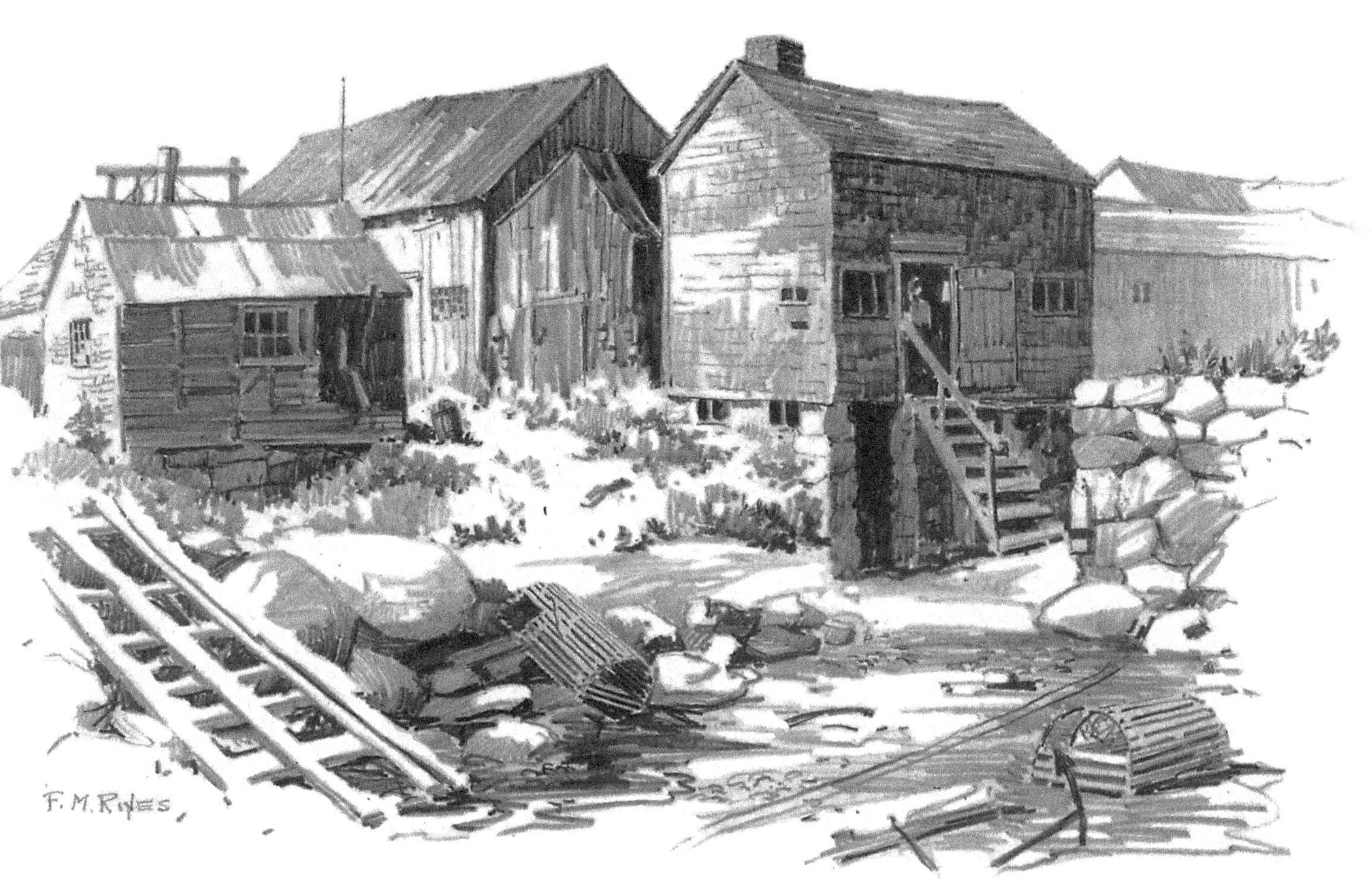

The points brought out here would apply equally well, if the drawing had been made from the actual subject instead of from the photograph.

STILL LIFE

"Still Life" subjects are always interesting. Any number of objects can be found in every home to provide material for such groups. Try to have objects that offer contrast in shape, size and color, arrange them carefully and as in outdoor scenes, have a strong lighting, in order to secure definite lights and shadows.

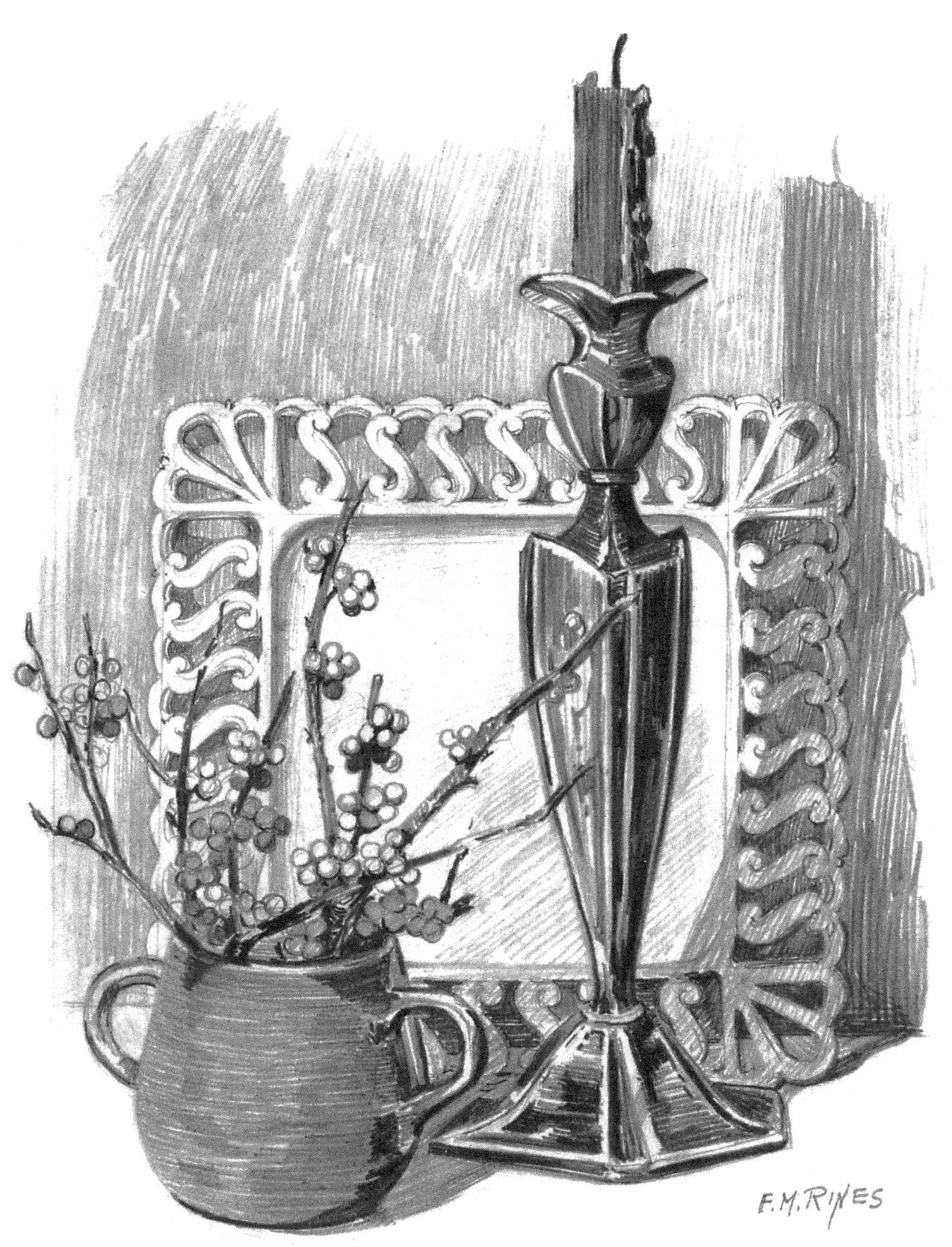

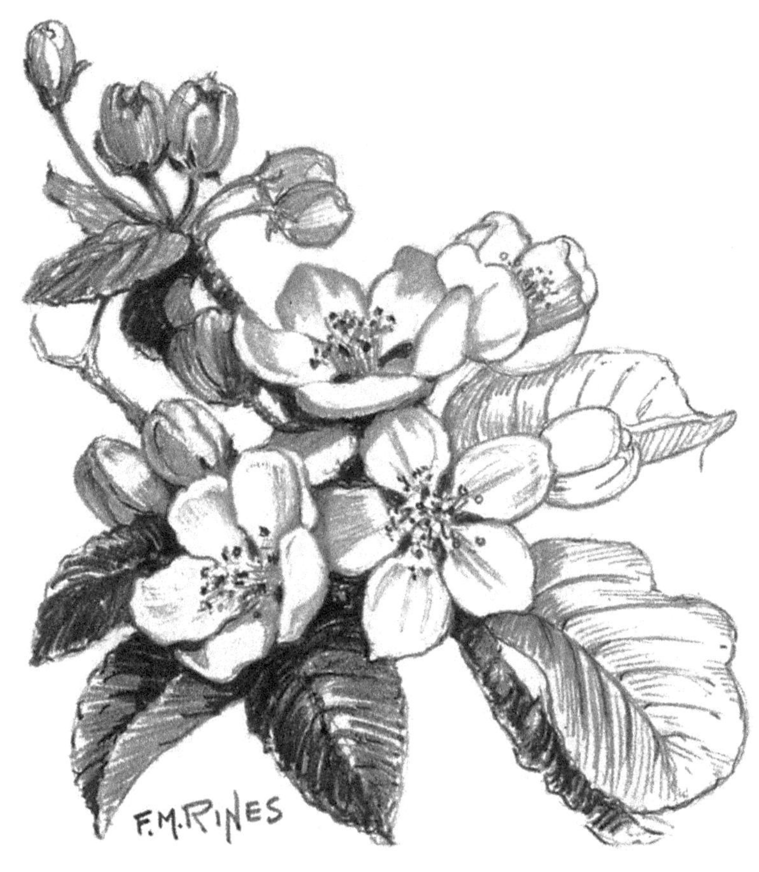

FLORAL TECHNIQUE

Subjects such as these are often available and offer excellent opportunities to practice drawing and technique.

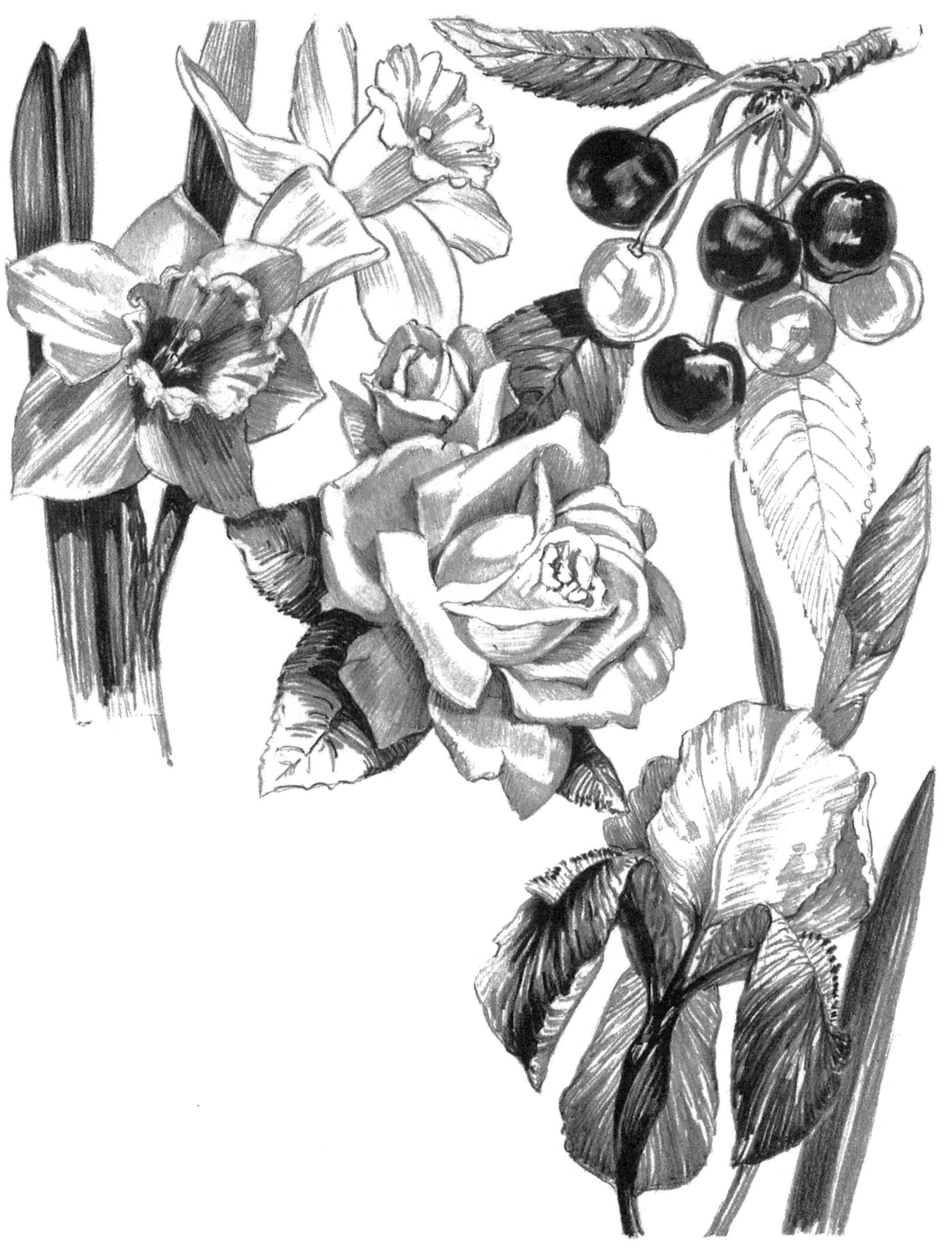

CONTRAST OF LIGHT AND SHADE

Notice the delicate light foliage. It is sometimes sharply silhouetted and some-times lost against the gray tones of the building. (It was drawn very carefully in outline, first.) Against the sky, the other tree (upper left) is darker. The different planes of the rocks have been suggested by strokes which vary in their direction.

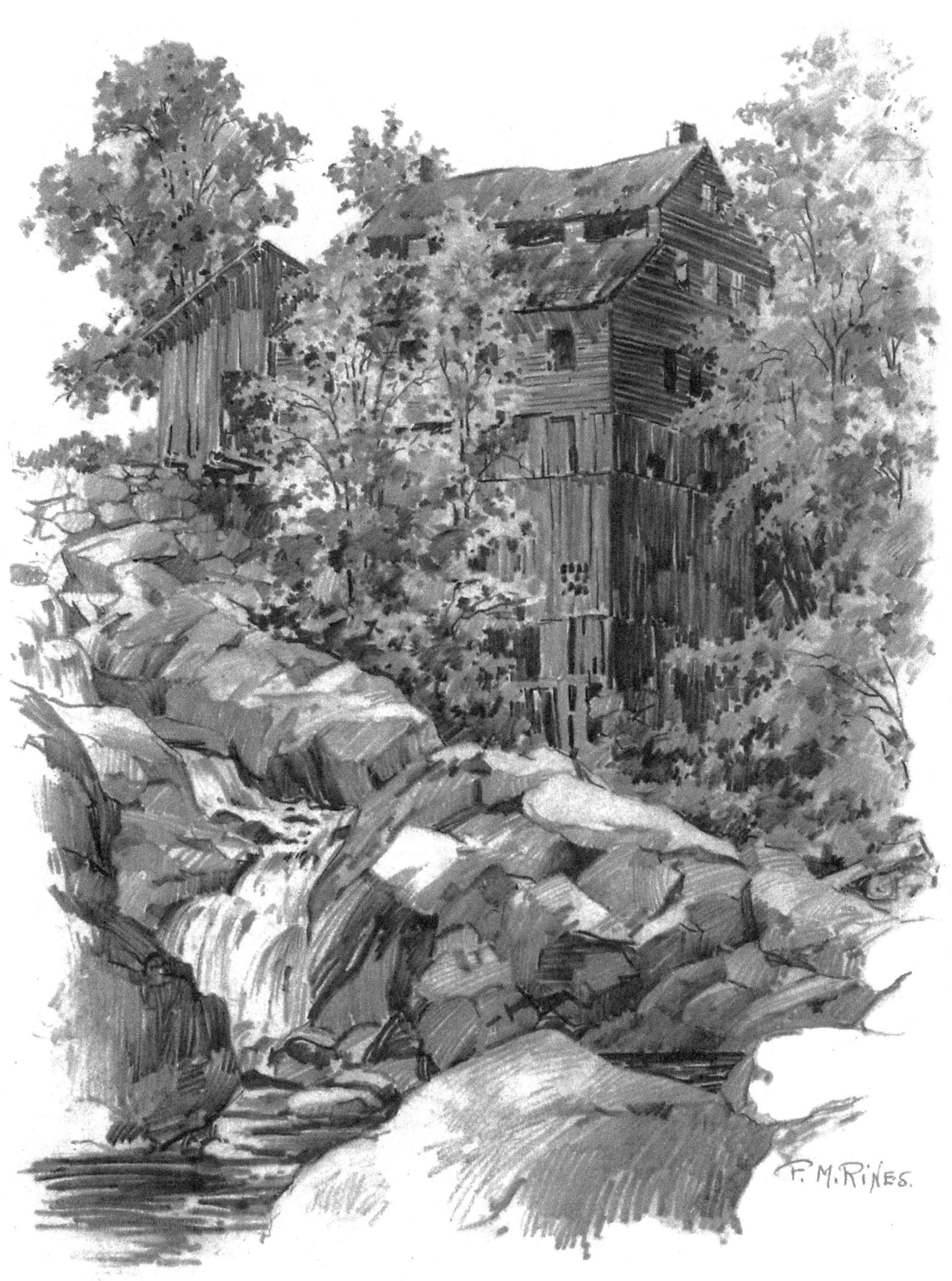

F. M. Rines.

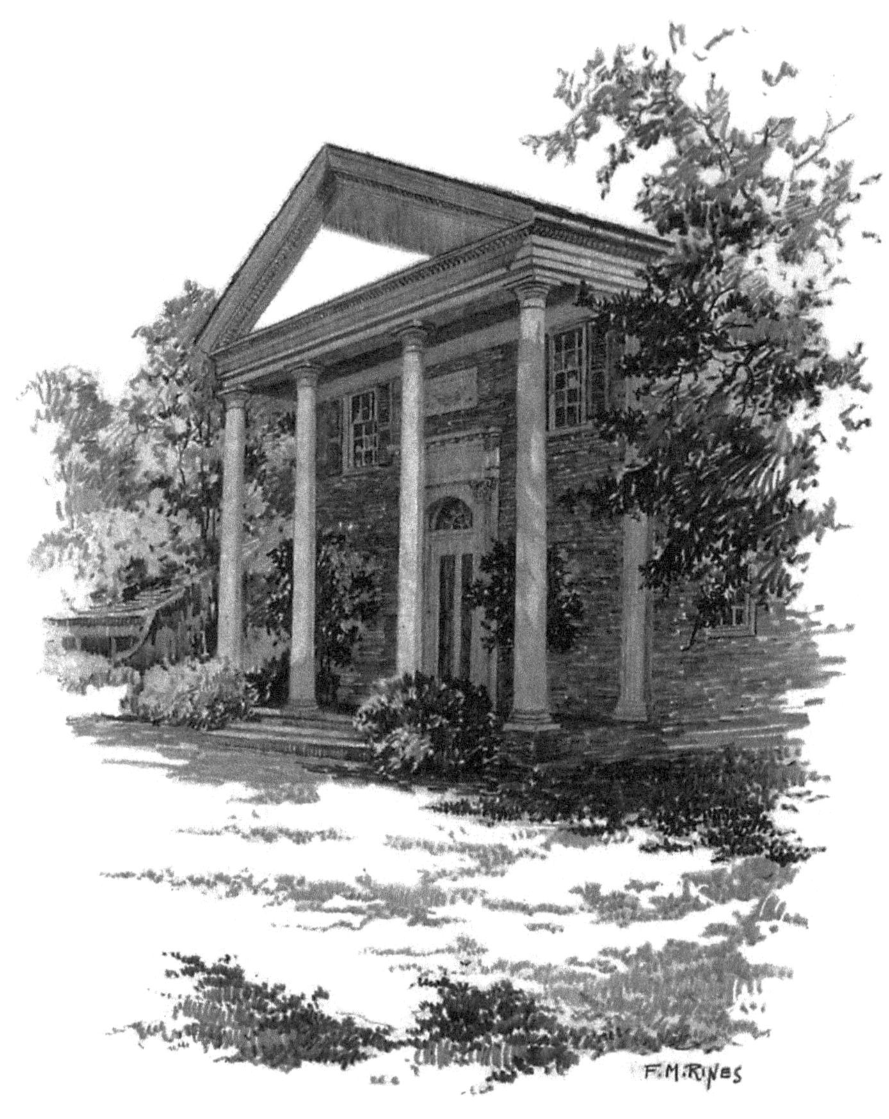

INTERESTING TEXTURES

This drawing, and those on the two following pages, serve to further demonstrate some of the principles mentioned in the preceding pages. The one on this page is especially interesting because of its perspective. The one on the next page shows some interesting textures. The last one illustrates how to treat different foliage masses in their relation to one another.

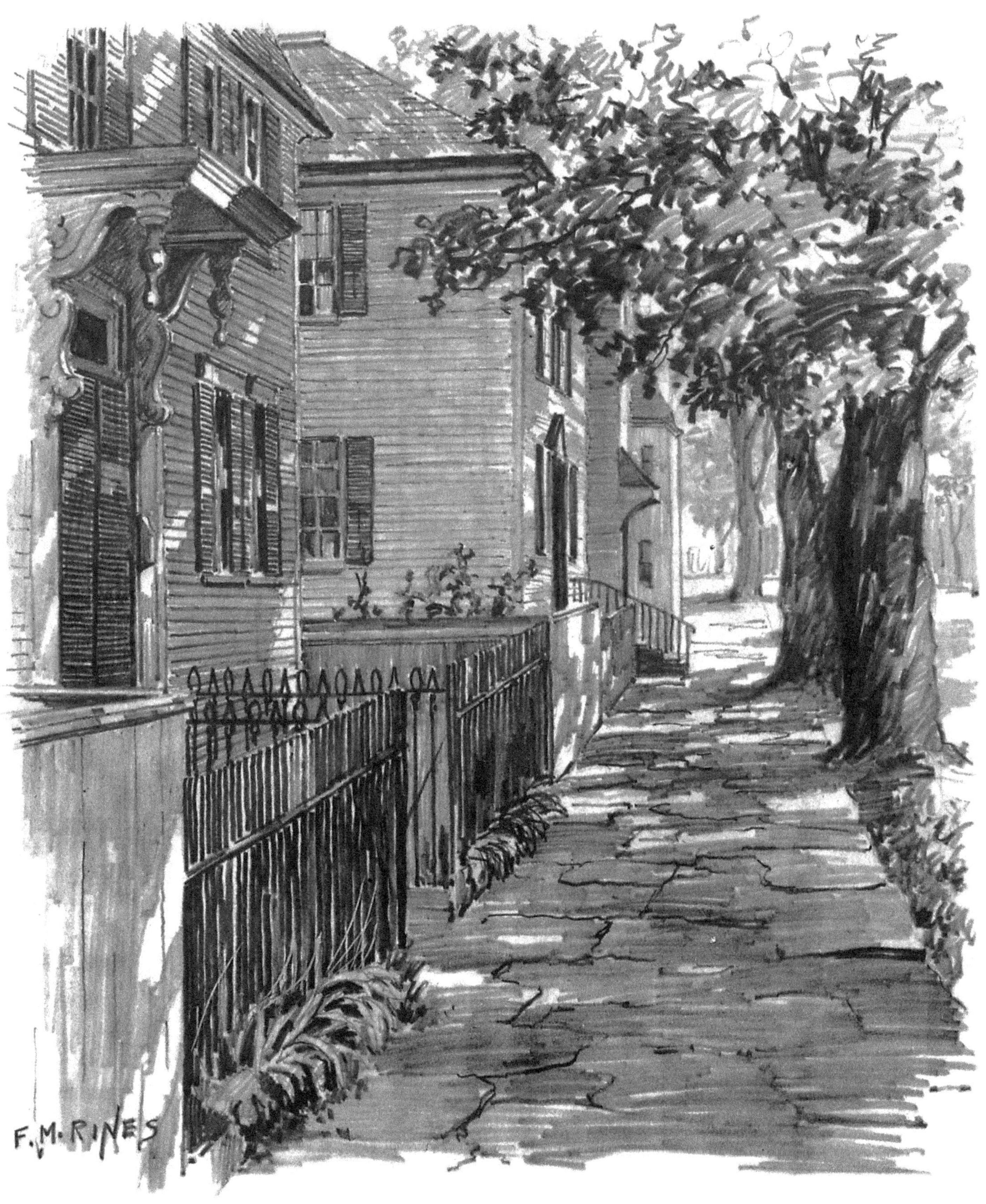
F. M. RINES

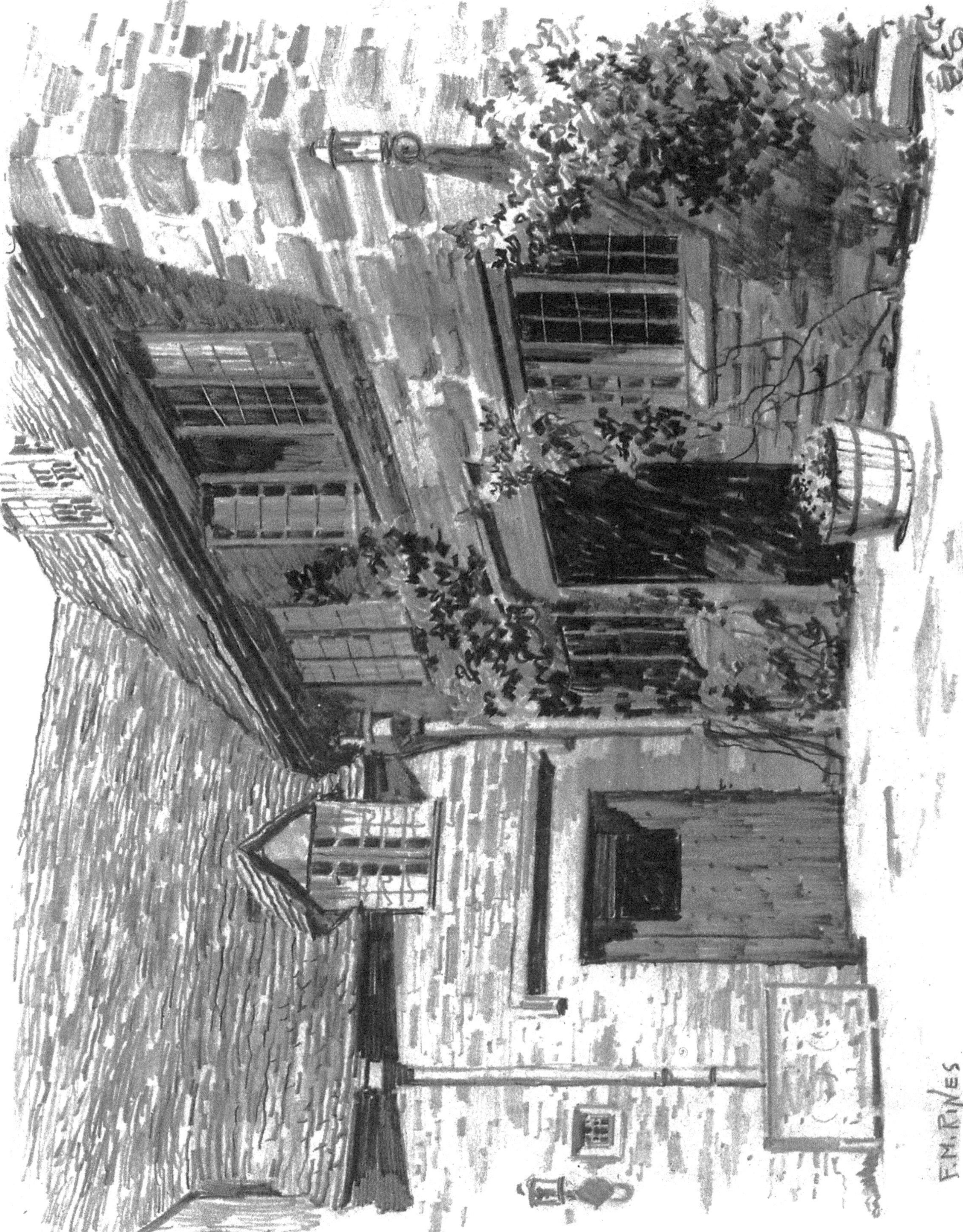

A PASTORAL SCENE

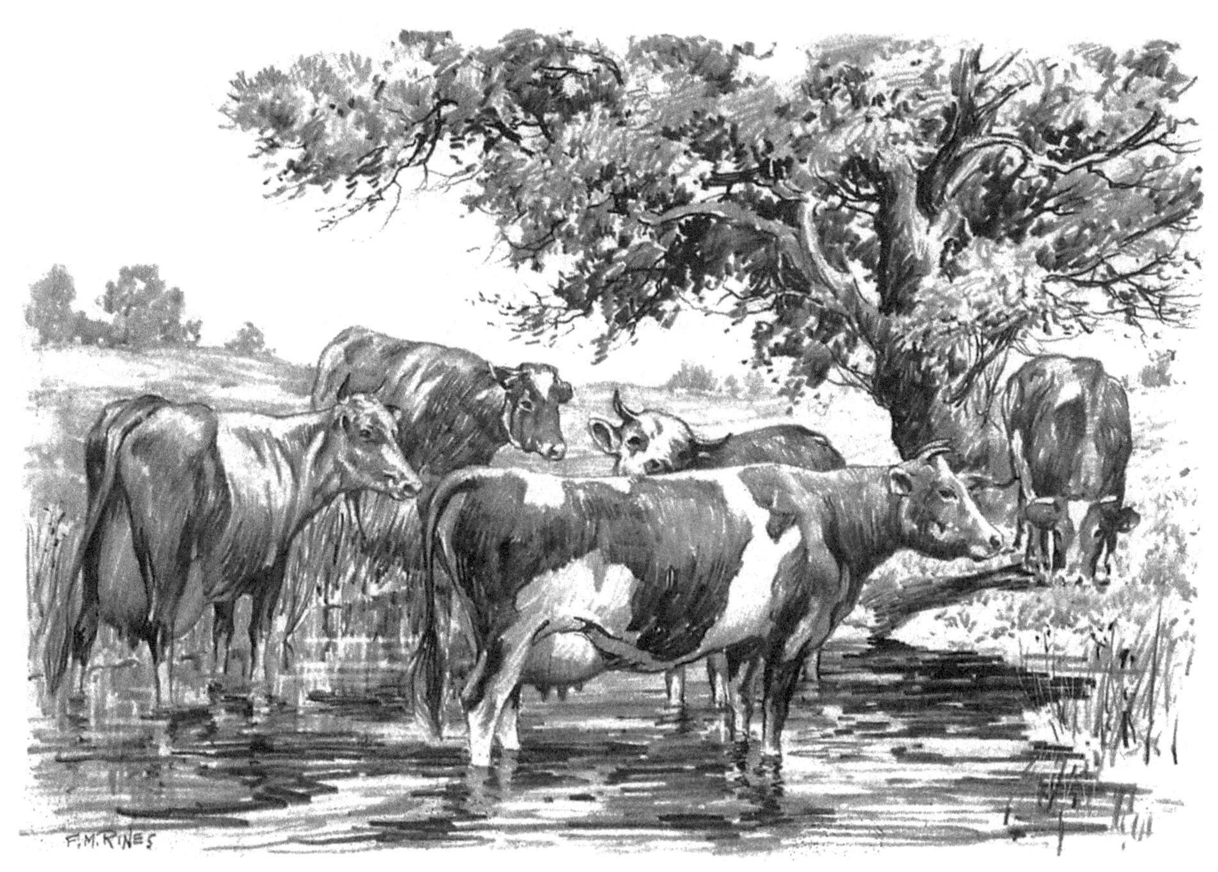

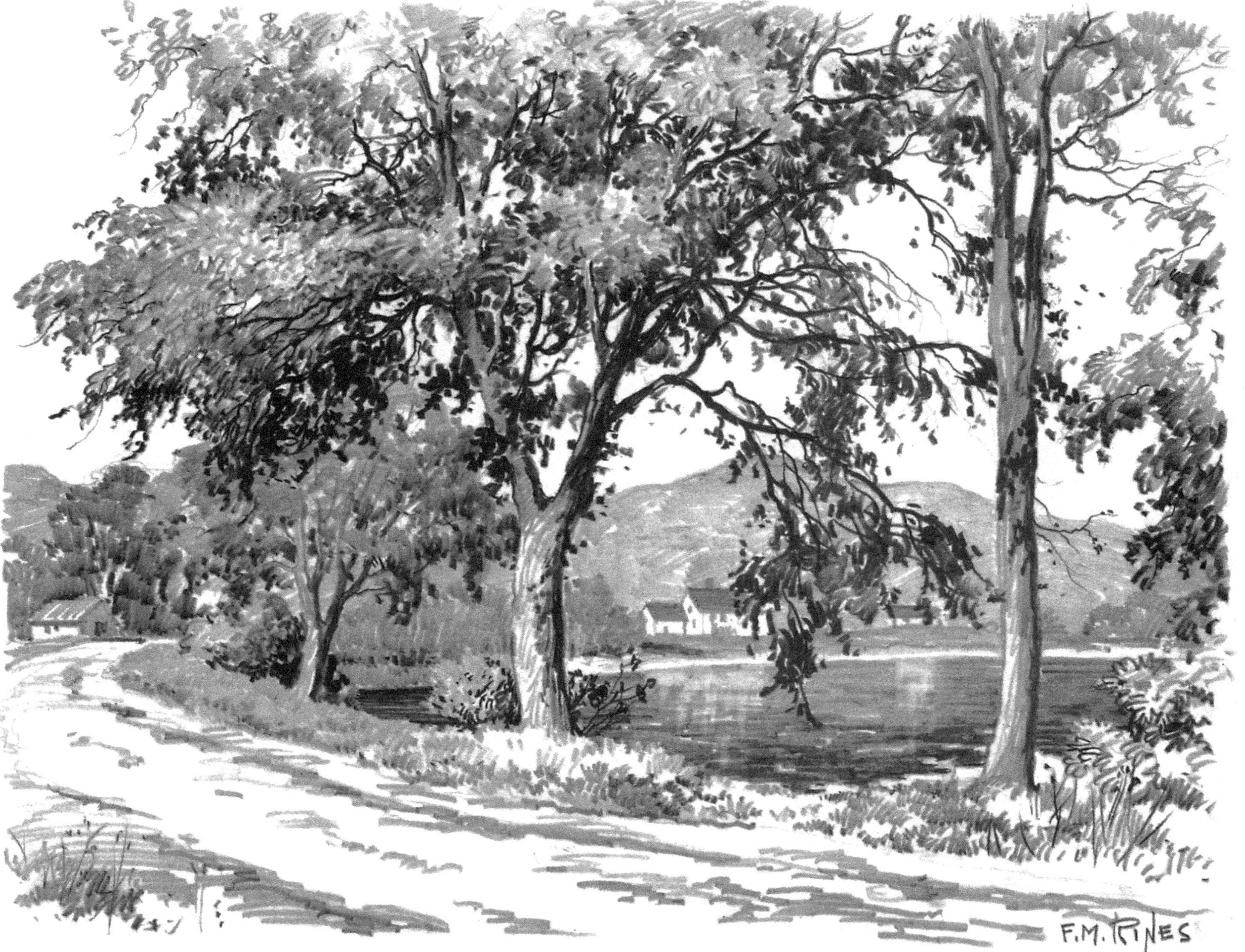

F.M. Rines

PENCIL SKETCHES

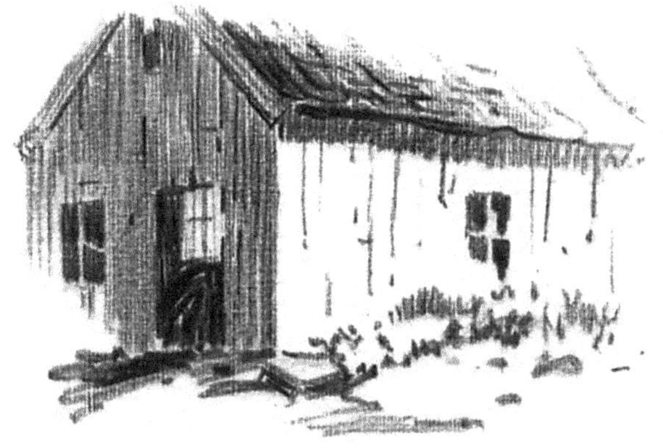

SUGGESTIONS

THE drawings from which the plates in this series were made are of a more elementary nature than those in "Drawing in Lead Pencil", a previous book by Mr. Rines. They are planned for the use of Junior High and High School students, but should be of equal benefit to others to whom the use of the pencil, as an artistic medium, is unfamiliar.

Besides the subjects presented here, photographs clipped from magazines, as well as those which the student may take himself, should be tried. In doing this, however, it must be borne in mind that one cannot draw all that the camera or the eye sees. Simplification is the keynote of any successful drawing, in any medium. Constant reference to the accompanying drawings should be made, in order to keep the above principle in mind, as well as for suggestions on how to render different materials.

A firm, white paper with not too rough a surface is necessary, and at least two pencils; one fairly hard and one fairly soft. A third, very soft pencil, helps greatly. Have a hard eraser, and if possible, a piece of "kneaded" eraser, also.

Use the hard pencil, with a long, sharp point, for sketching in lightly the outlines of the drawing. The other two pencils should have rather stubby points, flattened on a piece of sandpaper to an angle of about 45 degrees, in order to produce as wide a stroke as possible. Afterwards, wear the hard pencil down in the same manner. In this way, two or three different tones of wide strokes may be obtained. Use a firm pressure at all times; otherwise the drawing will have a woolly, smudgy appearance.

Always keep an extra sheet of paper or two under the one upon which you are drawing, in order to prevent the grain of the board from affecting the pencil strokes. Also use a piece of scrap paper under your hand, to avoid smudging the parts of the drawing already done.

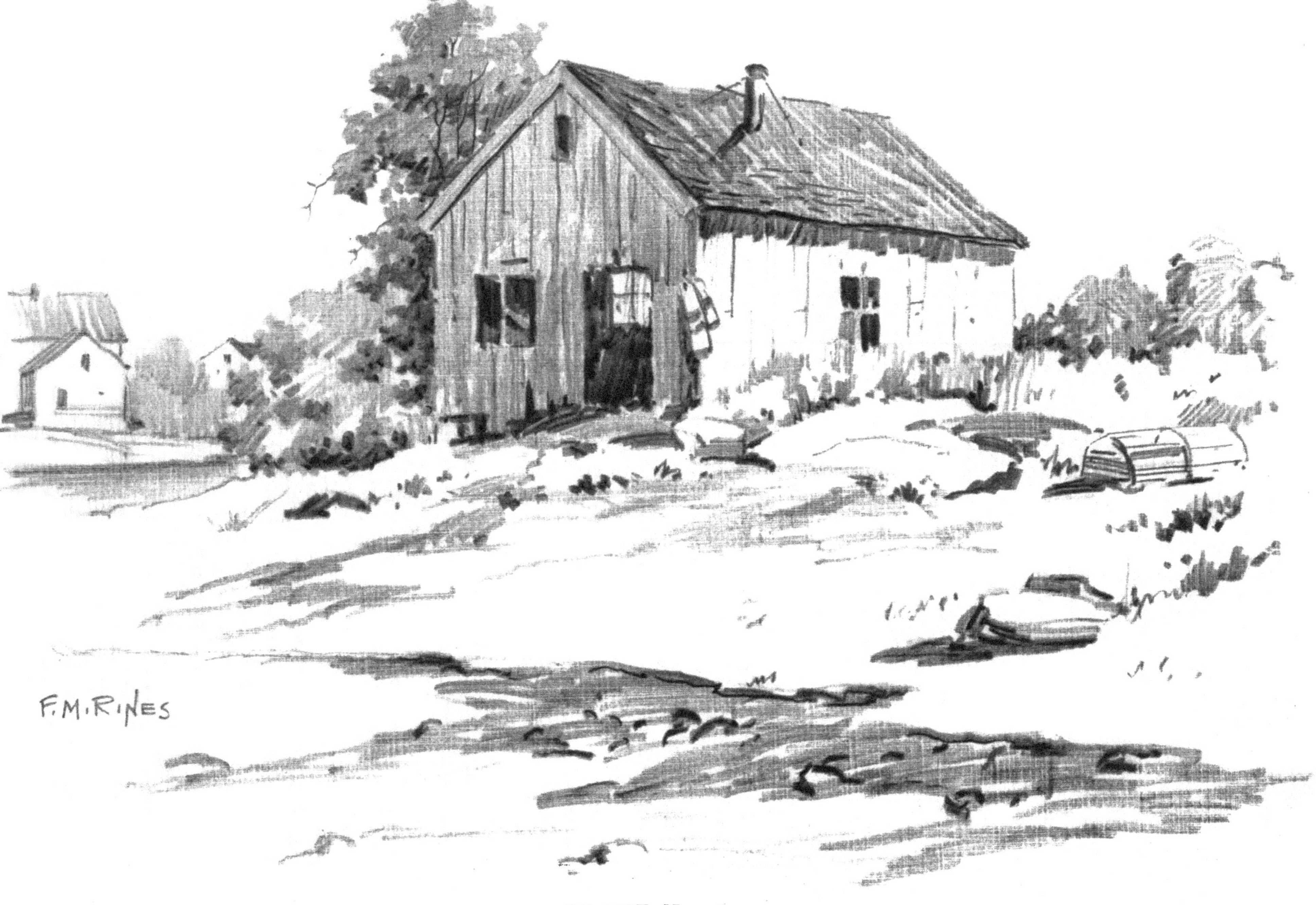

PLATE No. 1

The objective in this drawing, as in most of the others in this series, is to leave as much white paper as possible. A few lines to represent boards on the light side of the building are sufficient. A few sweeps of the broad edge of the lead, running in the general direction of the slope of the ground, indicate sunshine on the sandy beach better than a lot of pencil strokes would do. The same thing applies to the dark mud flats in the foreground. A few accents for stones or rocks may be added.

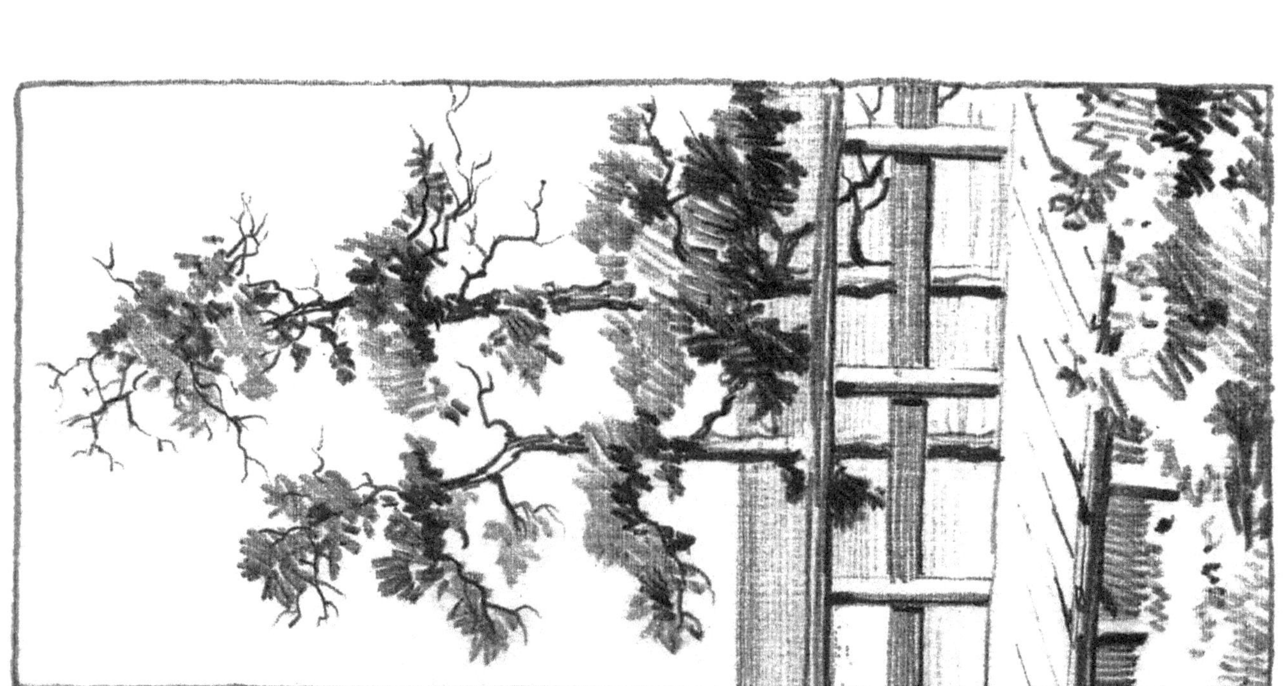

PLATE No. 2

In the picture on the left the contrast of the masses of the Pine foliage and the fine branches and twigs is the most interesting feature. In this drawing and in the one beside it, study very carefully the growth of the two kinds of trees, noticing particularly in the one on the right, the manner in which the smaller branches grow out from the main trunks.

Try making some similar drawings, either of trees seen from a window, or better still, from out of doors. Select a tree or trees which stand out against the sky and are not confused with others behind them.

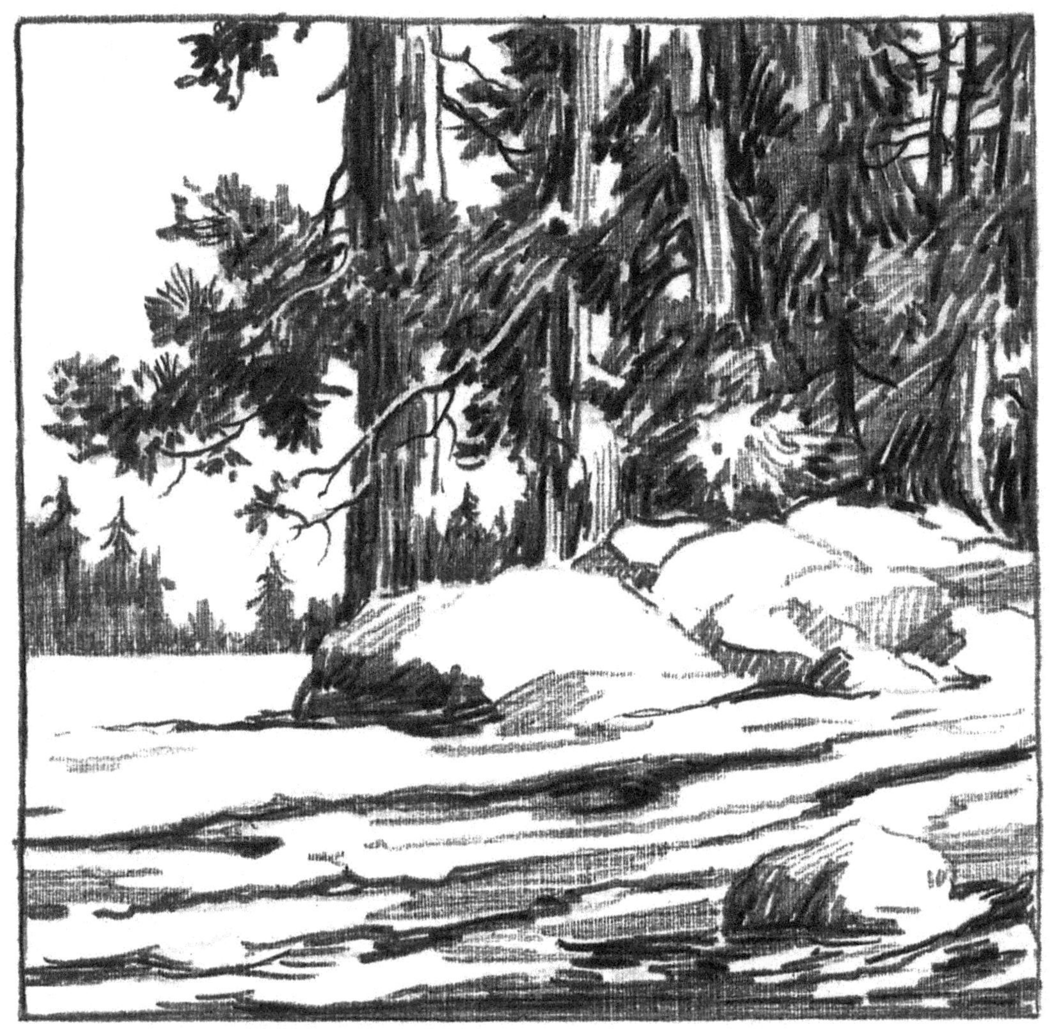

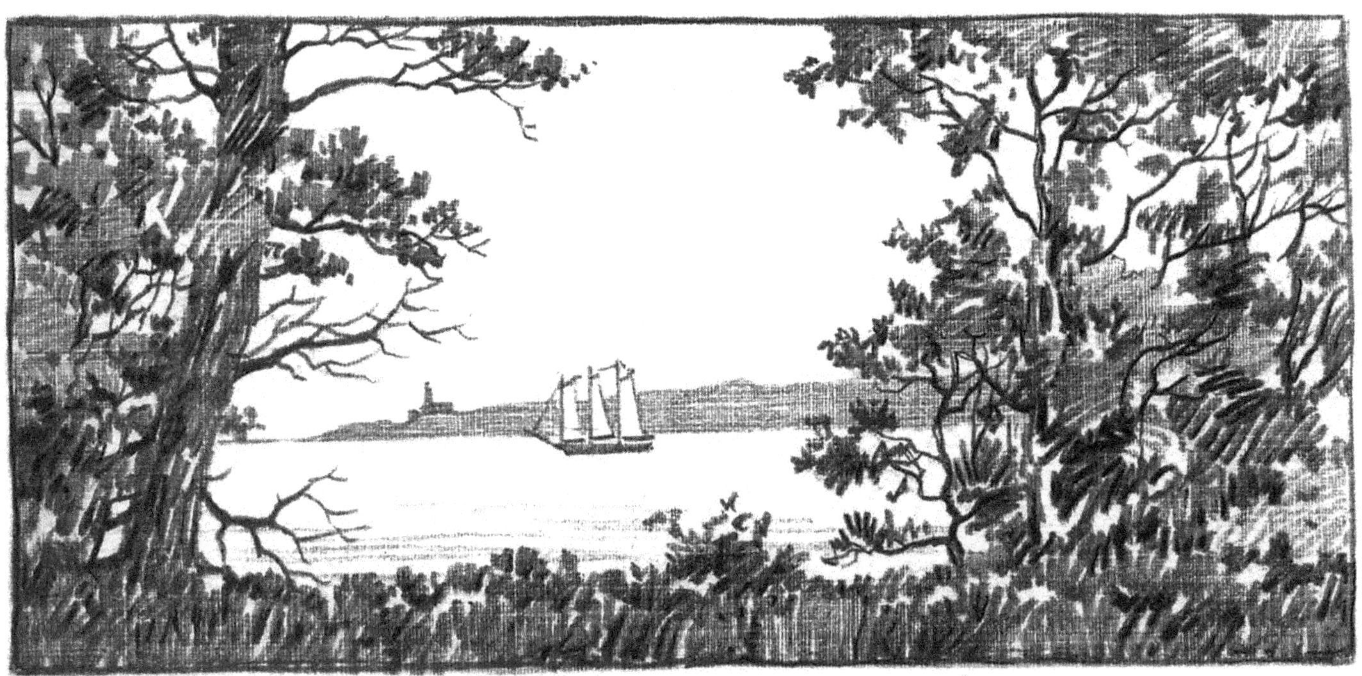

PLATE No. 3

In the upper picture, the heavy, broad strokes of the foliage suggest its dark green color and serve to make the white paper in the rocks and water stand out in contrast. The direction of the lines in the water indicates its movement.

The lower picture is almost, but not quite, a silhouette. Just enough difference in direction of stroke and variety of tone has been used to suggest the various masses and kinds of foliage. Keep the ship, water and distant shore line very simple, in order to push them into the background.

PLATE No. 4

In the drawing of the Elm tree, observe how different are the strokes representing foliage, from those in some of the other drawings for boards, clapboards, shingles, etc. Be sure to get a dark and light side to the tree, and to leave some white masses of foliage. Doing this keeps the tree from appearing flat, or in other words, gives it three dimensions instead of only two.

Drawing the windmill is not as difficult as it might seem. The only new problem is in fading off part of the topsails. This prevents too much attention being attracted away from the mill itself, and keeps the drawing from becoming a picture of the sails instead of the building.

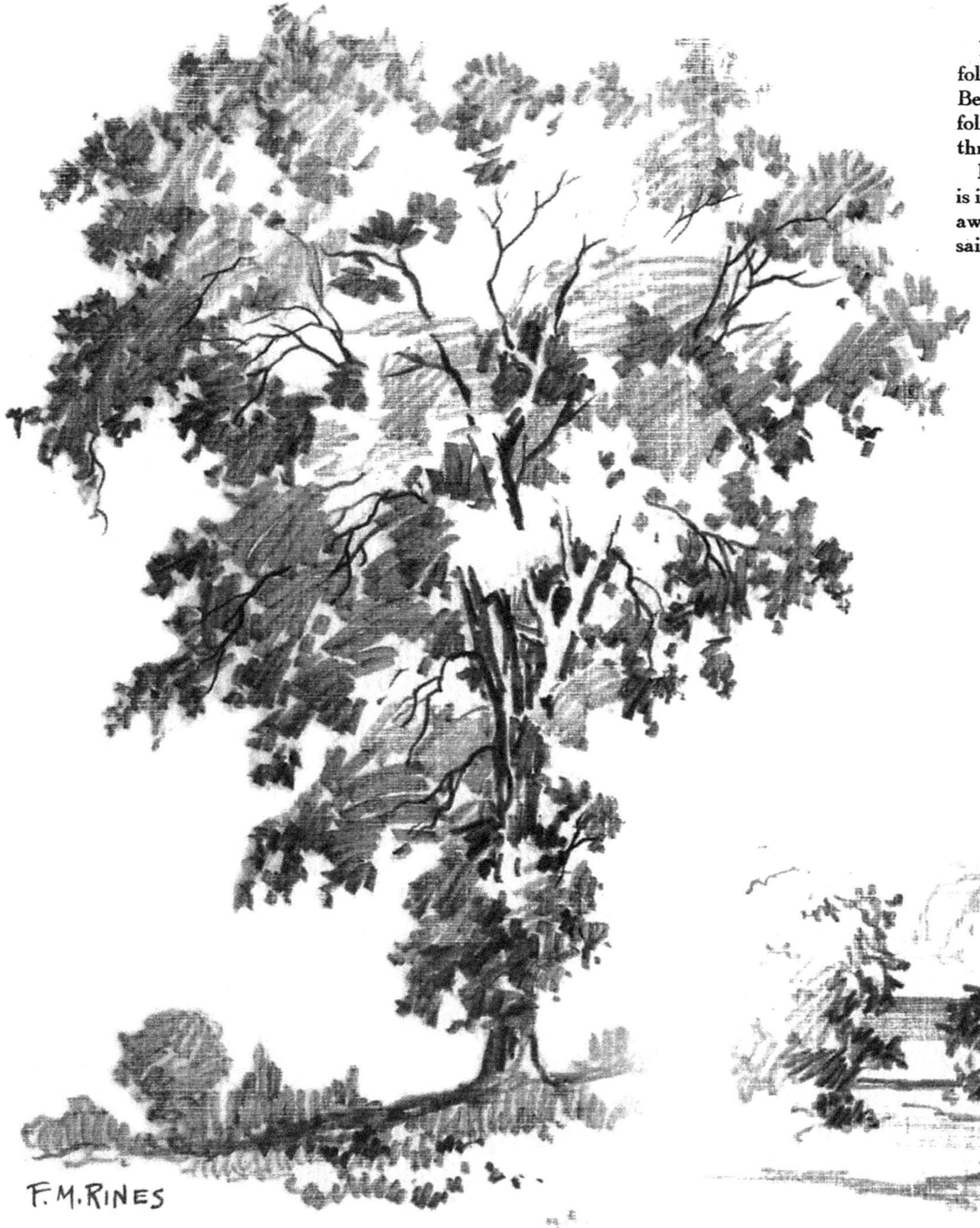

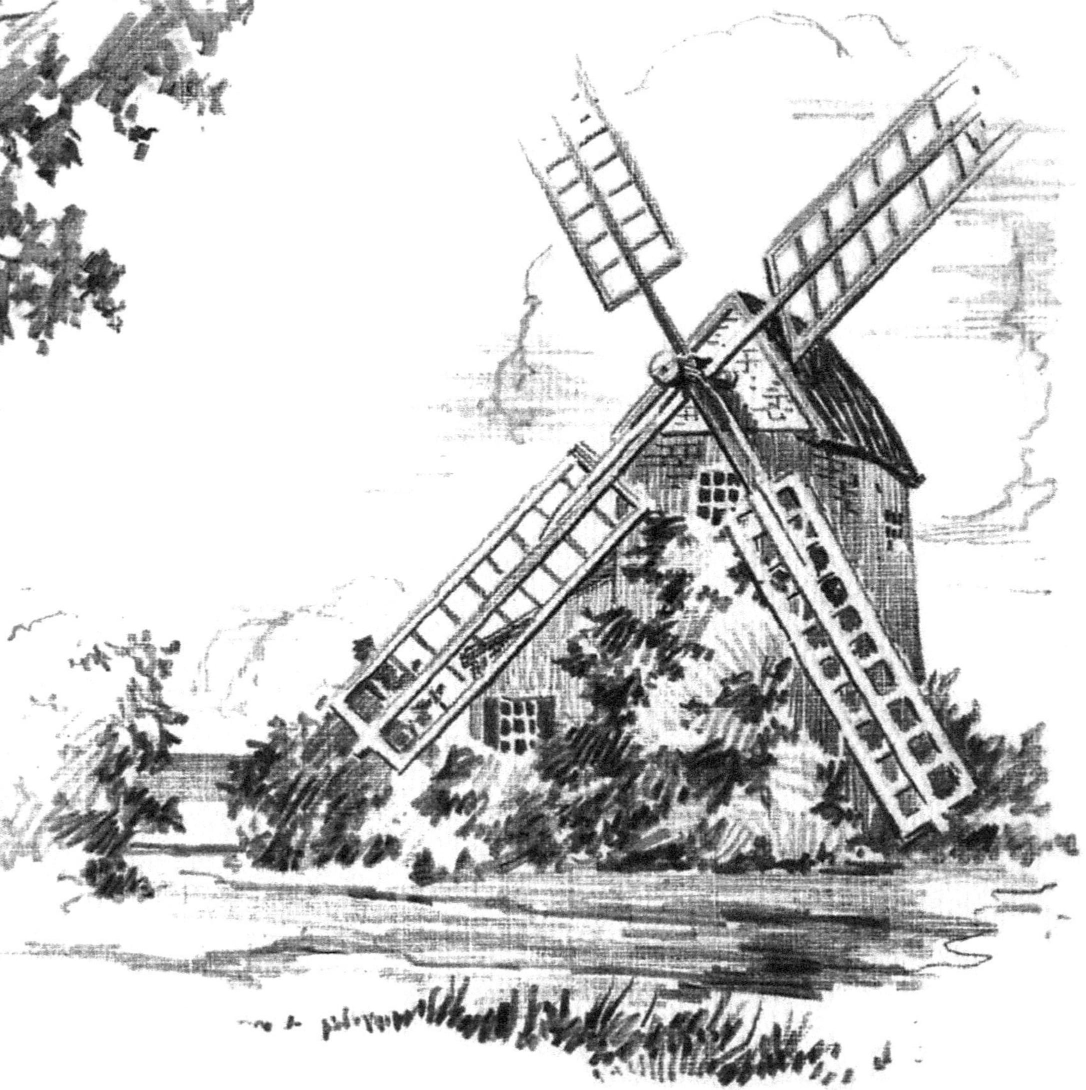

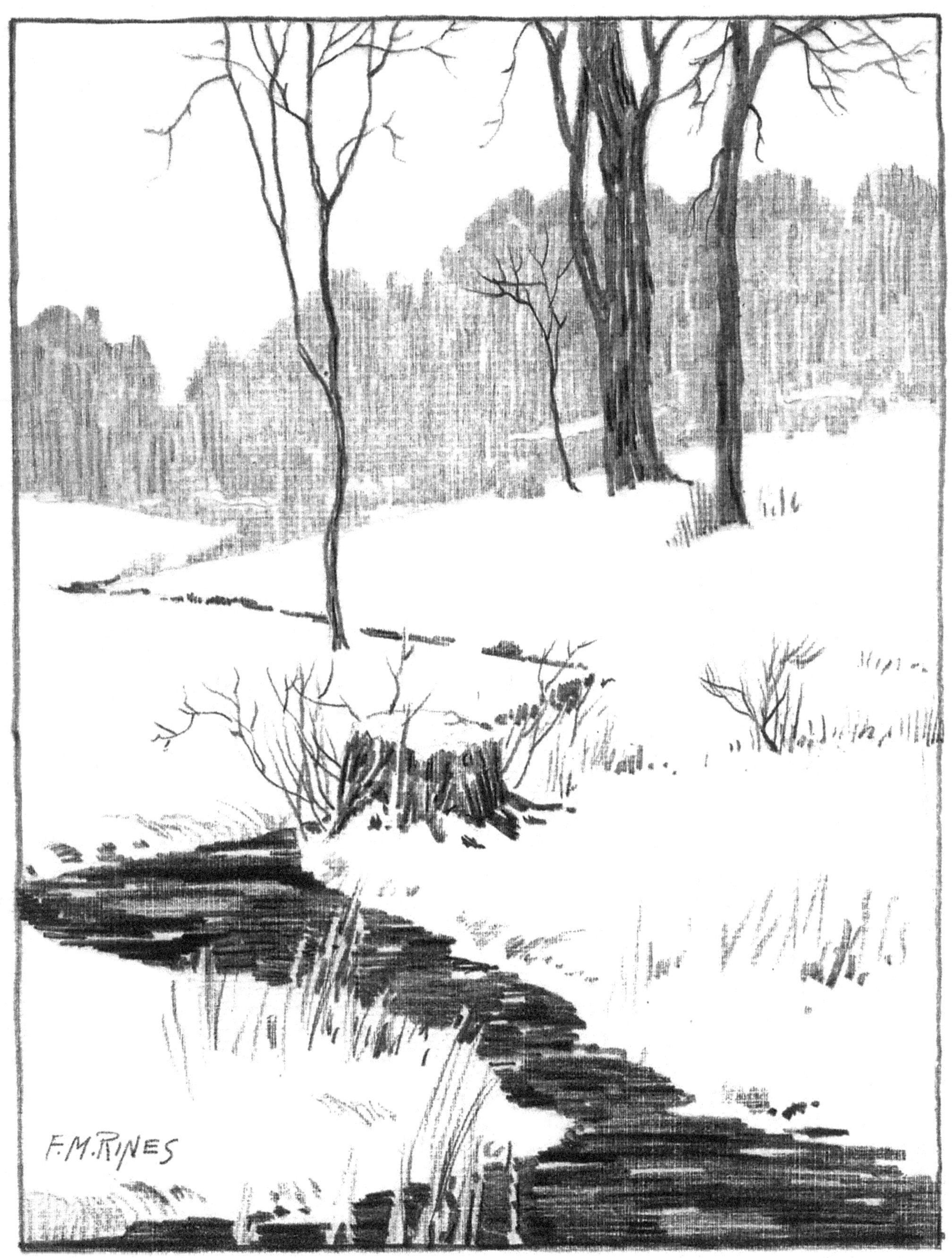

PLATE No. 5

The blackness of the water and the few bare twigs and reeds serve to emphasize the whiteness of the snow. The light vertical strokes of the background represent a simplified way to indicate distant woodland. Study carefully the placing and the construction of the trees, and notice that each one is of a different girth, or diameter.

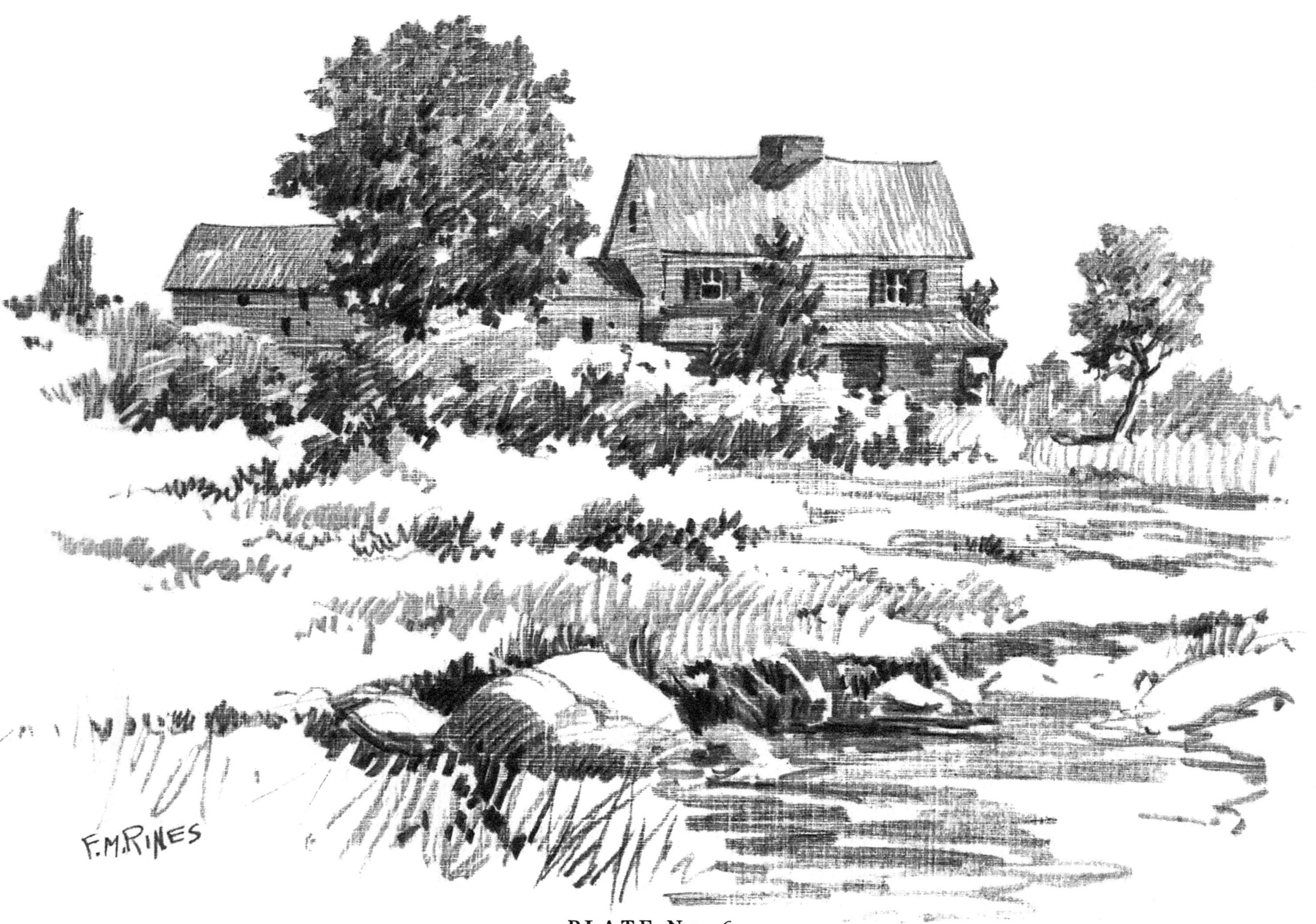

PLATE No. 6

The house and the tree in this scene are all in shadow. Notice, however, the difference in direction of the strokes on the roofs, the sides of the house and in the tree, which keeps them from becoming monotonous. As in most of the other drawings, a mass of grass, shrubbery, etc., is simplified into some dark accents against the white paper, contrasting the foreground with the background. The horizontal lines in the water are again different from those of the rest of the drawing.

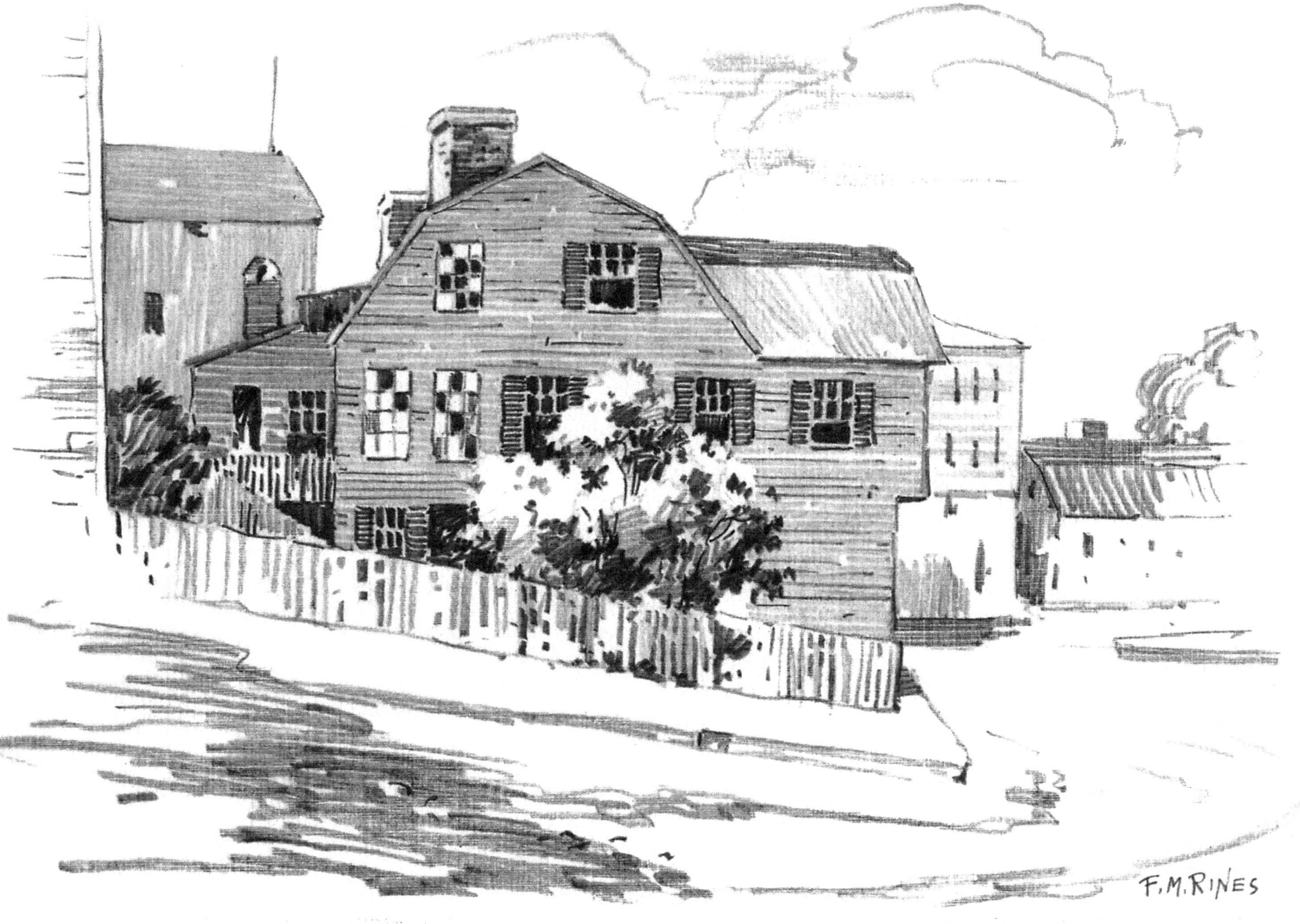

PLATE No. 7

Horizontal, rather wide strokes of the pencil, many of the strokes kept separate to show white streaks between them, represent clapboards. Afterwards, add a few accents with the sharp edge of the pencil. The bush, partly white paper and partly dark strokes, stands out from the gray tone of the house. A few vertical strokes of varying width are enough to indicate the fence.

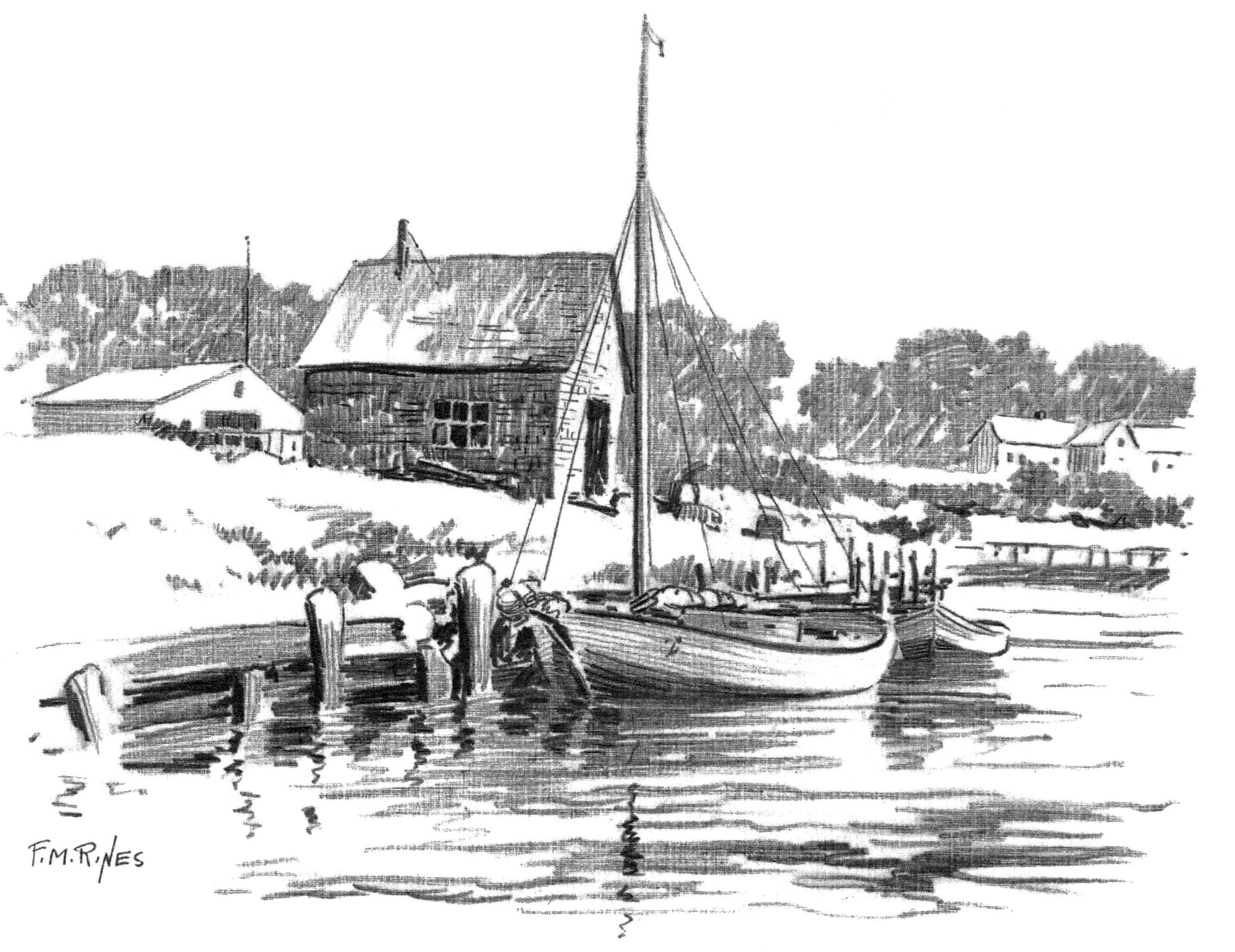

PLATE No. 8

Notice how the background of trees is suggested by broad lines, all about the same tone, but changing somewhat in their direction.

The shingles on the shadow side of the building are made with short vertical strokes, with a few sharp horizontal accents. The roof partly white paper and partly gray tone, affords more variety than would one all white or all gray.

Here again, some horizontal lines suggest water and a few wigglely vertical lines the reflections of the piles and the mast of the boat.

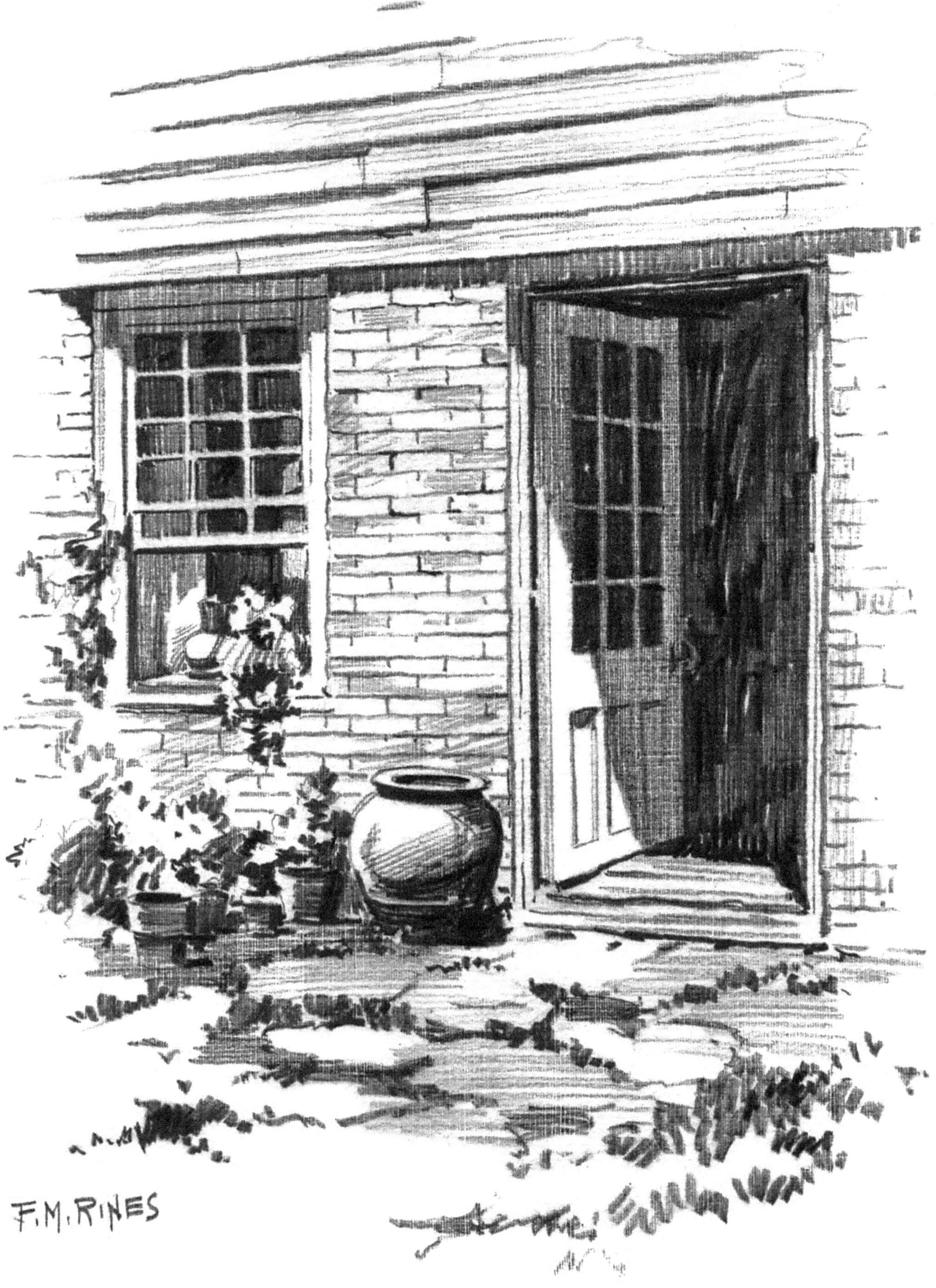

PLATE No. 9

This drawing affords an interesting study of the rendering of different textures. While the general tendency of the black strokes of the open doorway is toward the vertical, they have been varied just enough to prevent them from appearing too mechanical.

Try making a drawing of your own front or back door, keeping in mind the problems presented in this drawing.

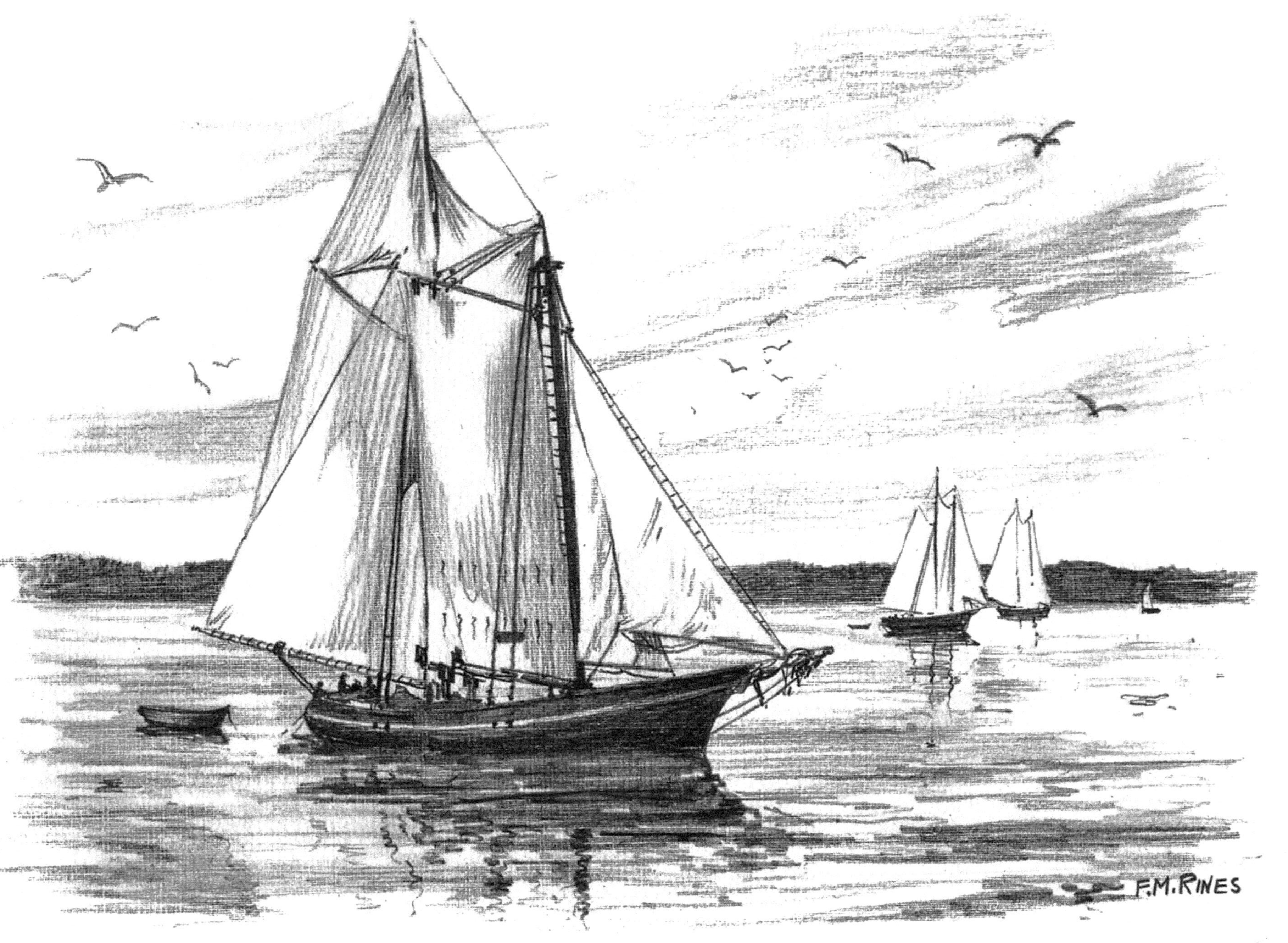

PLATE No. 10

Take especial care in making this drawing that the schooner is not placed in the center of the picture. A few light tones in the sky break up what otherwise would be too large an expanse of white. The gray tones on the sails serve the same purpose.

Be sure, when indicating water in any picture, to have the strokes either absolutely horizontal or vertical, otherwise the water will not appear to be level.

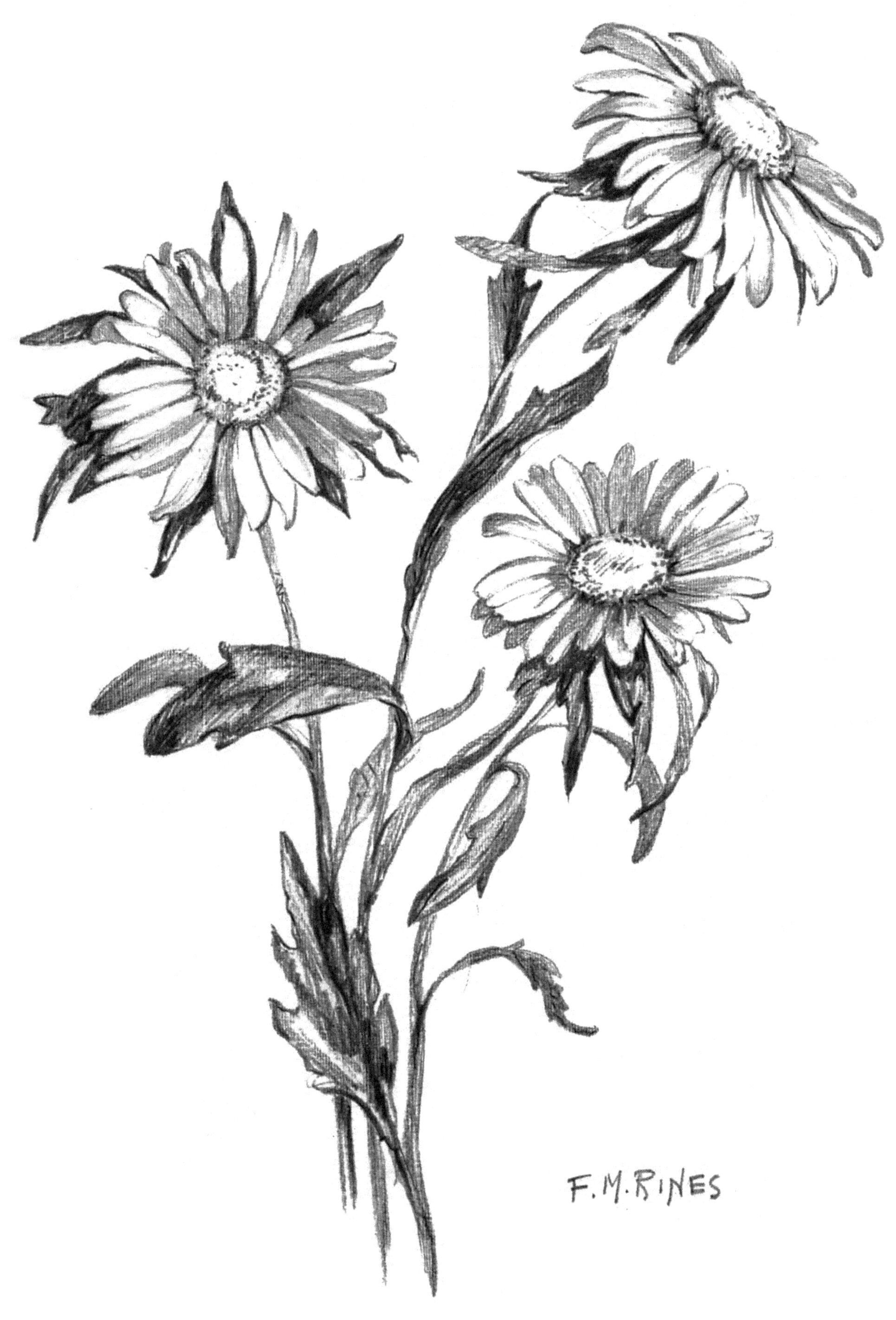

PLATE No. 11

After drawing these flowers, try some similar subjects of your own selection. Choose flowers that offer a contrast of light blossoms and dark leaves, or the reverse, and do not, at first, make too complicated an arrangement.

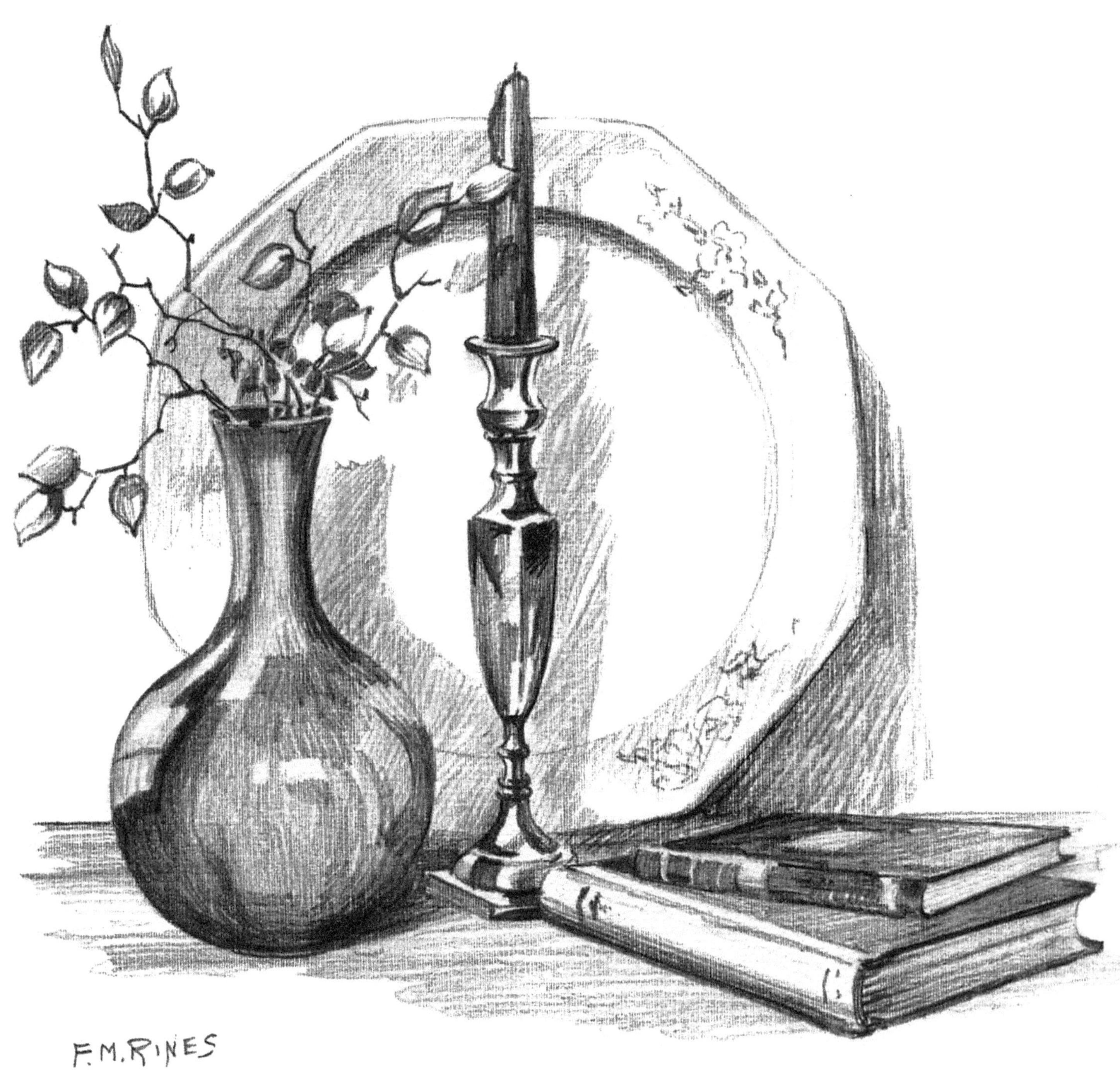

PLATE No. 12

As in the flower drawing, any number of subjects similar to this still life study may be arranged. Select objects offering plenty of contrast in form and size, and in light and shade, as well as color. Let the direction of your strokes be determined largely by the contour or direction of the surface you are rendering. Notice, in this drawing, the curved strokes used on the vase and the straight ones on the candlestick.

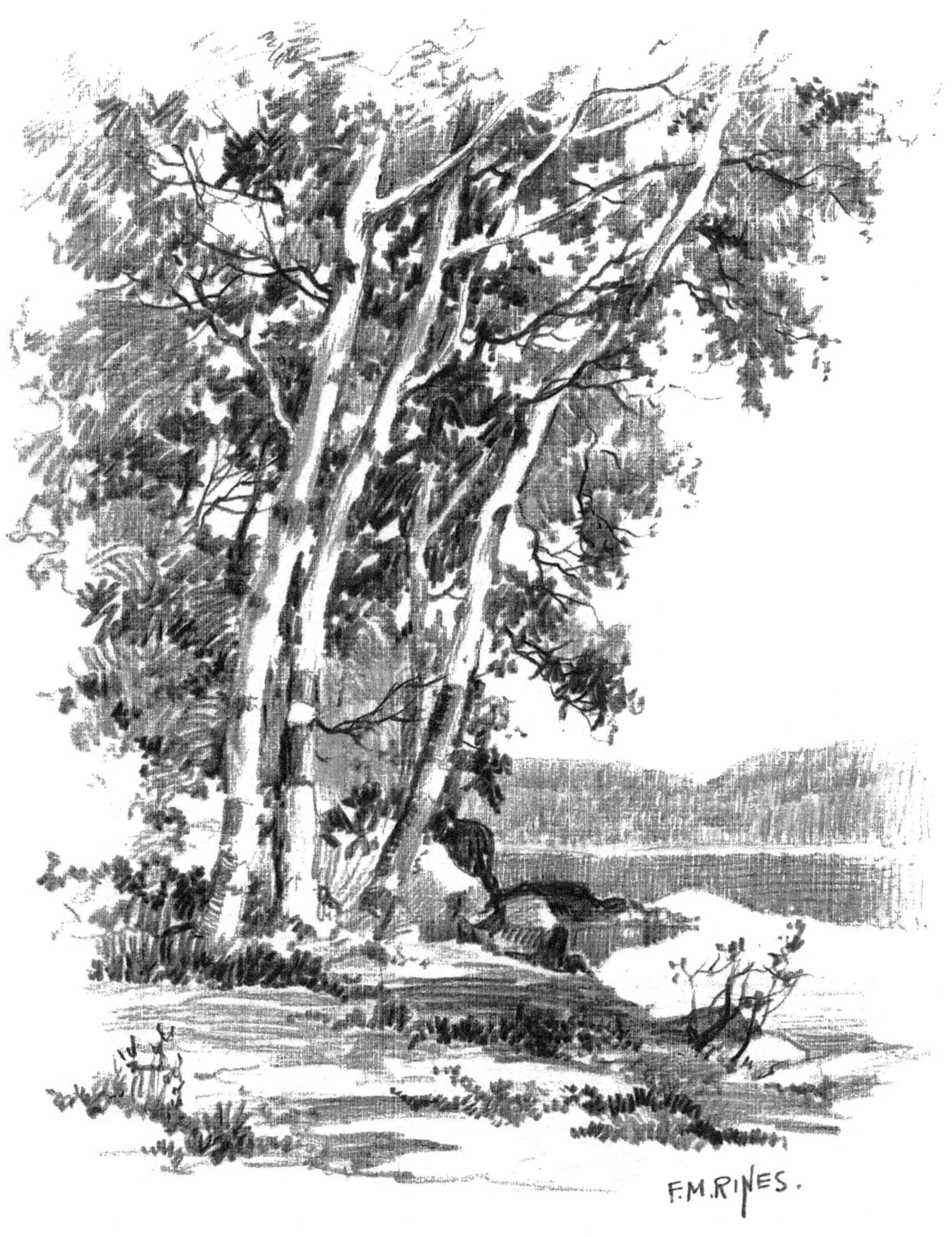

PLATE No. 13

Draw very carefully the white trunks of these Birch trees. Then work the tones of the foliage around them, varying the direction of the strokes, so that the trunks stand out as white paper against them. Afterwards, tone down the trunks a little and add the branches and twigs.

The method of drawing the background is similar to that described elsewhere. Suggest some grass and dirt in the foreground.

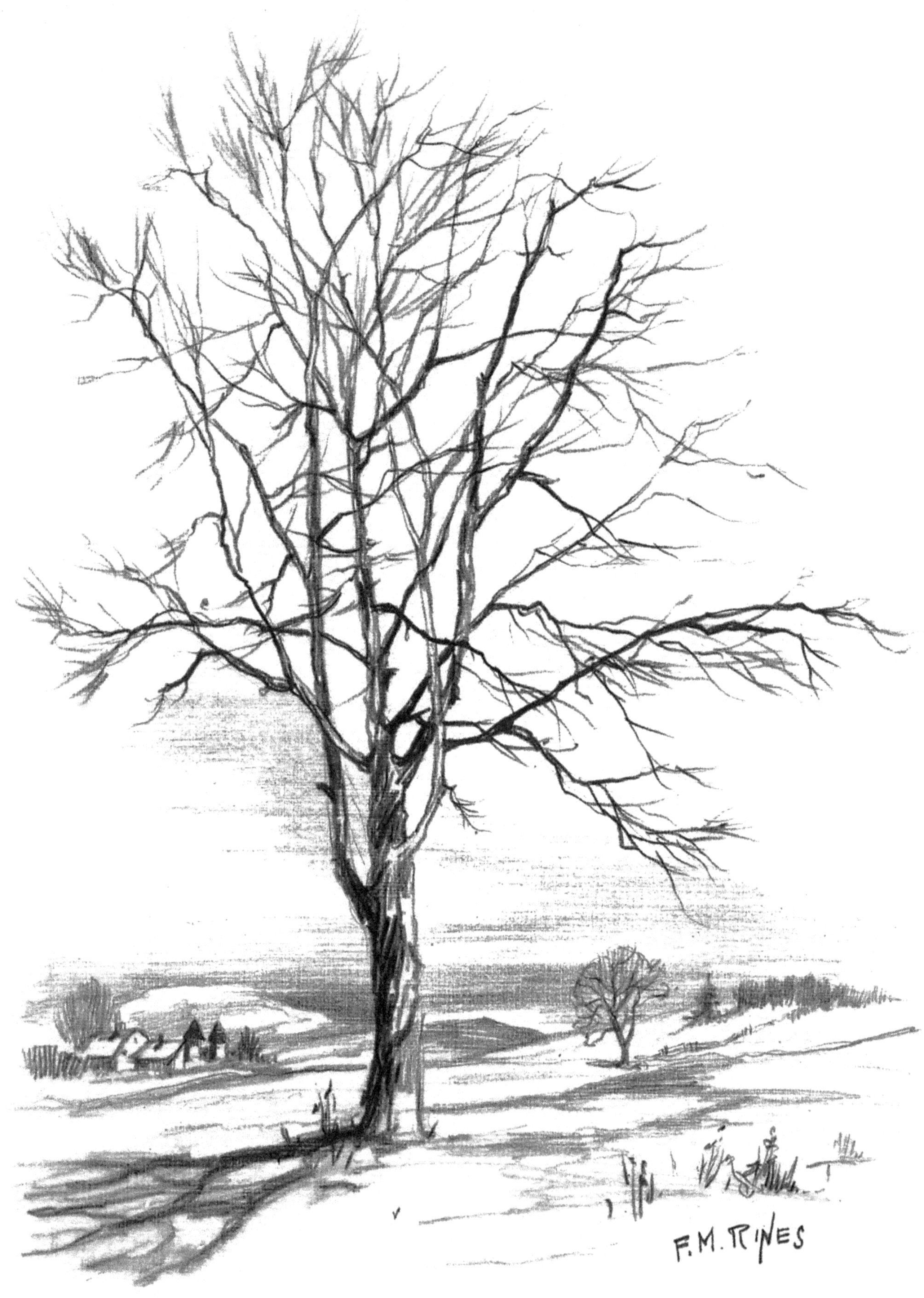

PLATE No. 14

In this study of a Maple tree in winter, sketch in lightly the trunk and main branches; then go over these lines and accent some of them. Next add the twigs and finer branches. Notice particularly how the smaller branches grow out from, or join, the larger ones.

Observe how different is the growth of the branches, as well as the silhouetted shapes of various species of trees.

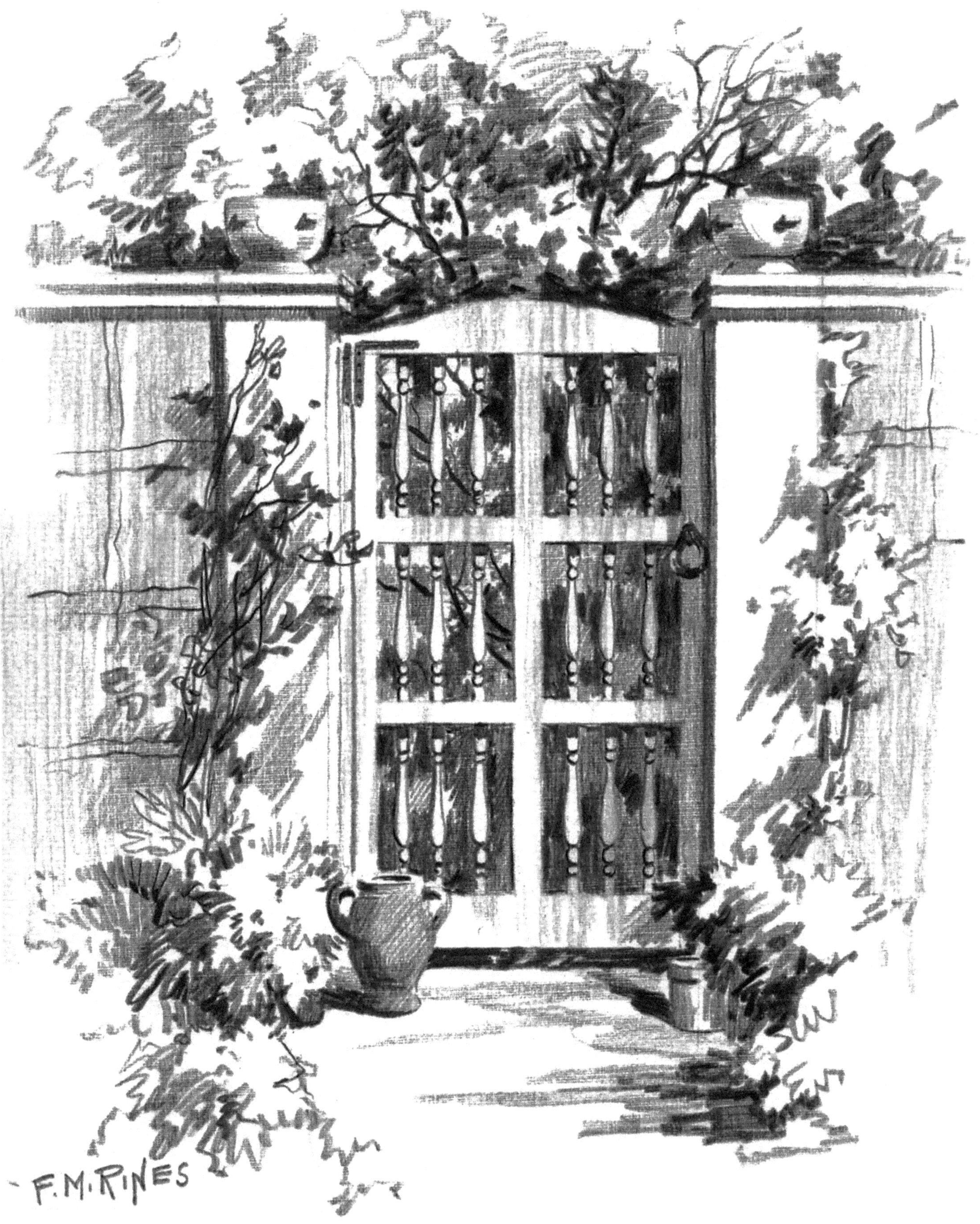

PLATE No. 15

Draw the gateway very carefully in outline, with the hard pencil; especially the spokes. Be very exact as to their spacing.
When this has been done, darker and lighter tones of the foliage behind them will help to make them stand out.
The vines and low shrubbery may be indicated with broad, sketchy lines.
The last stage is to run a few light lines with the hard pencil, over the gate and wall, to relieve the whiteness of so much paper.